Great Taste ~ Low Fat

ONE-POT MEALS

TIME
LIFE
BOOKS

ALEXANDRIA, VIRGINIA

TABLE OF CONTENTS

Introduction *4*

Secrets of Low-Fat Cooking *6*

Pork and Three-Pepper Stew

page 24

Soups & Stews

Bouillabaisse *11*

Louisiana Beef Stew with Dumplings *13*

Beef Goulash *14*

Peppery Fish and Corn Chowder *16*

Split Pea Soup with Smoked Turkey *17*

Mixed Shellfish Stew *19*

Country-Style Chicken Fricassee *21*

Cuban-Style Beef Stew *22*

Beef and Barley Soup *23*

Pork and Three-Pepper Stew *24*

Chicken and Mushroom Stew *27*

Curried Pork Stew *28*

Moroccan Chicken Stew with Lemon *29*

Quick Beef Chili *30*

Italian Pasta-Vegetable Soup *33*

Coq au Vin *34*

Skillet Dinners

Seafood-Sausage Paella *36*

Chicken-Fried Steak Dinner *38*

Couscous with Chicken and Vegetables *39*

Skillet Antipasto Dinner *41*

Stir-Fried Beef and Vegetables with Orzo *42*

Hot and Tangy Shrimp *45*

Pork "Un-Fried" Rice *47*

Ham and Sweet Potato Sauté *49*

Broccoli and Potato Frittata *50*

Fish Roll-Up Supper *53*

Chunky Chicken and Vegetable Hash *54*

Skillet Spaghetti and Meatballs *57*

Spicy Rice with Chicken and Vegetables *58*

Lamb Meatballs with Spinach Fusilli *61*

Beef Pilaf *63*

Chicken with Peanut Sauce *64*

Pork and Butternut Squash Sauté *66*

Milanese-Style Rice *68*

Oven Dinners

Roast Chicken Dinner *71*

Baked Rigatoni with Vegetables *72*

Open-Face Eggplant and Pesto Sandwiches *75*

Baked Salmon on a Bed of Vegetables *77*

Pork with Potatoes and Artichokes *78*

Meat Loaf Blue Plate Special *79*

Chicken Enchiladas

page 85

Creamy Penne, Bacon, and Vegetable Bake *80*

Hearty Cassoulet *82*

Chicken Enchiladas *85*

Paper-Wrapped Chicken and Vegetables *86*

Vegetarian Moussaka *89*

Golden Chicken and Corn Casserole *90*

Asparagus Strata *93*

Turkey Orloff Casserole *94*

Wagon Wheels with Spinach-Basil Sauce *97*

Ham and Scalloped Potatoes *98*

Tuna-Noodle Bake *100*

Cod Fillets in Parchment *102*

Pies & Pizzas

Chili Pie *105*

Shepherd's Pie *106*

Potato-Topped Turkey Pie *107*

Greek Spinach and Feta Pie *108*

Vegetable Pot Pie *111*

Rustic Pizza *113*

Ground Beef Pasties with Chutney Sauce *114*

Beef Pot Pie in Phyllo *117*

Pork and Apple Pot Pie *119*

Stromboli *121*

Mexican-Style Pizza *122*

Rice-Crusted Quiche Lorraine *125*

Deep-Dish Pan Pizza *127*

Tamale Pie *128*

Cooking for a Crowd

Barbecue-Sauced Steak with Vegetable Kebabs *130*

Three-Bean Vegetable Chili *133*

Stuffed Manicotti with Ham and Cheese *135*

Green Chili with Pork *136*

Baked Beans and Pork Chops *137*

Pastitsio *139*

Chicken in a Pot *141*

Broccoli-Mushroom Lasagna *143*

Choucroute Garni *144*

Spaghetti with Chunky Turkey Sausage Sauce *145*

Peasant-Style Beef Stew *147*

Creole Turkey and Rice Stew *149*

Southern-Style Shrimp Boil *150*

Swedish Meatballs *153*

Glossary *154*

Index *157*

Credits *159*

Metric Conversion Charts *160*

INTRODUCTION

Our mission at Great Taste~Low Fat is to take the work and worry out of everyday low-fat cooking; to provide delicious, fresh, and filling recipes for family and friends; to use quick, streamlined methods and available ingredients; and, within every recipe, to keep the percentage of calories from fat under 30 percent.

Without a doubt, a meal in one pot has a lot going for it: ease of preparation, quick cleanup, and the age-old appeal of needing nothing but a piece of crusty bread to make it a hearty supper. Unfortunately, most traditional one-pot meals belong to a place and time where they could be poked and tended for the better part of a day, and where an abundance of fat was of no concern.

For most of us, those days are long gone, but the allure of the one-pot meal lingers. In this hurried, harried age, a successful "one-pot meals" cookbook needs the following: Every recipe must have the appropriate balance of protein, starches, and vegetables for a complete meal; the recipes must be streamlined, requiring little or no advanced preparation; the book should provide a variety of cooking methods, ingredients, and presentations; and every recipe must be delicious, filling, and low in fat.

With many thanks to our wonderful chefs, we are happy to say that Great Taste~Low Fat *One-Pot Meals* has met and, in many cases, even exceeded, our goals.

VARIETY

The title "One-Pot Meals" may conjure up a vision of a huge pot of soup or stew, simmering on top of the stove—and indeed, these warming, robust suppers make up our first chapter, Soups & Stews. We follow with Skillet Dinners, which includes sautés, stir-fries, frittatas, chicken-fried steak, paella, and more. Oven Dinners presents additional variety, with casseroles (both familiar and innovative), an asparagus "strata," chicken enchiladas, salmon fillets baked on a bed of vegetables, and a pork roast with potatoes and artichokes, to name a few. We return to the oven with the next chapter, Pies & Pizzas, with delicious fillings in a stunning array of imaginative crusts, from mashed vegetables to tortillas to ready-made doughs, and even rice. And for those of you who love to entertain (or just want leftovers), our last chapter, Cooking for a Crowd, is dedicated to big batches suited for fuss-free entertaining, including two chili recipes, lasagna, and gumbo.

Admittedly, some of these dishes require more than one pot to prepare, but the vast majority are served from one vessel, thereby helping with cleanup and avoiding last-minute juggling. And you may notice that we've exceeded our usual "30 minutes or less" working times for some of our dishes. The reason for this is simple and unavoidable: When you cook all the parts of a meal in one recipe, it takes more time.

LOW-FAT STRATEGIES

Our chefs believe that low-fat cooking needn't be complicated. Indeed, it can even be easy, with the right instruction. Fat does many things for food: It insulates tender meats, distributes flavor, and holds ingredients together—all of which are essential to a superior one-pot meal. To that end, our chefs use a few techniques that, when correctly employed, will produce the desired results; low fat without compromise. Some are very basic (using a nonstick skillet and lean ingredients) and some come from the chefs' years of experience (the judicious use of fats, flavor enhancers, and dairy products). These techniques are, of course, explicitly written into each recipe—no prior cooking experience is necessary. In the "Secrets of Low-Fat Cooking" section on the following pages, there are suggestions that will help you not only with our recipes but in all of your cooking. And whenever a recipe has an unusual technique or a slightly tricky procedure, we've provided an illustrated tip for you.

One-pot meals have a twofold attraction: One is for the happy diner, who enjoys well-blended flavors and a satisfying meal; the other is for the cook, who is freed from meal planning. With *One-Pot Meals*, you can simply relax and enjoy the feast.

CONTRIBUTING EDITORS

Sandra Rose Gluck, a New York City chef, has years of experience creating delicious low-fat recipes that are quick to prepare. Her secret for satisfying results is to always aim for great taste and variety. By combining readily available, fresh ingredients with simple cooking techniques, Sandra has created the perfect recipes for today's busy lifestyles.

Grace Young has been the director of a major test kitchen specializing in low-fat and health-related cookbooks for over 12 years. Grace oversees the development, taste testing, and nutritional analysis of every recipe in Great Taste-Low Fat. Her goal is simple: take the work and worry out of low-fat cooking so that you can enjoy delicious, healthy meals every day.

Kate Slate has been a food editor for almost 20 years, and has published thousands of recipes in cookbooks and magazines. As the Editorial Director of Great Taste-Low Fat, Kate combined simple, easy to follow directions with practical low-fat cooking tips. The result is guaranteed to make your low-fat cooking as rewarding and fun as it is foolproof.

NUTRITION

Every recipe in *Great Taste-Low Fat* provides per-serving values for the nutrients listed in the chart at right. The daily intakes listed in the chart are based on those recommended by the USDA and presume a nonsedentary lifestyle. The nutritional emphasis in this book is not only on controlling calories, but on reducing total fat grams. Research has shown that dietary fat metabolizes more easily into body fat than do carbohydrates and protein. In order to control the amount of fat in a given recipe and in your diet in general, no more than 30 percent of the calories should come from fat.

Nutrient	Women	Men
Fat	<65 g	<80 g
Calories	2000	2500
Saturated fat	<20 g	<25 g
Carbohydrate	300 g	375 g
Protein	50 g	65 g
Cholesterol	<300 mg	<300 mg
Sodium	<2400 mg	<2400 mg

These recommended daily intakes are averages used by the Food and Drug Administration and are consistent with the labeling on all food products. Although the values for cholesterol and sodium are the same for all adults, the other intake values vary depending on gender, ideal weight, and activity level. Check with a physician or nutritionist for your own daily intake values.

SECRETS OF LOW-FAT COOKING

ONE-POT MEALS

One-pot dishes are the perfect way to serve complete meals that are both healthful and delicious. All components of the meal are nutritionally accounted for and balanced within each recipe, including the protein (meat, fish, poultry, or cheese), the starch (potatoes, pasta, rice, or bread), and the vegetables. And unlike more traditional one-pot recipes, which require hours of simmering or baking, our recipes have been efficiently streamlined: They use readily available ingredients and a minimal number of cooking steps.

LOW-FAT TECHNIQUES

In any type of low-fat cooking, it is important to know how to replace the fullness, flavor, and "mouth-feel" that fat adds to dishes. The hearty carbohydrates that are included in many of the dishes here, from barley, rice, and pasta to potatoes, peas, corn, and beans are not only filling, but also provide flavor and texture. Tortillas and bread are another convenient, low-fat method of rounding out a dish and providing a sense of satisfaction.

To retain the creamy richness that high-fat dairy products can add to dishes, we've used reduced-fat alternatives. For example, we use low-fat yogurt, reduced-fat cream cheese, and evaporated low-fat

or skimmed milk. All of these foods add body, because they still have just enough fat to be satisfying. Buttermilk also lends a tangy depth of flavor in addition to body, as do puréed cottage cheese, part-skim ricotta, and reduced-fat sour cream. (We use low-fat buttermilk, even though it is slightly higher in fat than regular buttermilk, for the added richness.) And as for fat-free dairy products, nonfat yogurt is the only one we use because it does not compromise taste or texture.

The proper use of thickeners can also give the impression of a butter or cream sauce, but without the fat. Cornstarch mixed with a little liquid and stirred into a dish at the end of cooking creates a sauce with a light consistency. A simple white sauce made with flour and low-fat milk (and no butter) adds an appealing richness. Flour or cornstarch can also be used to stabilize sour cream and yogurt so that they will remain thick and creamy when they are heated.

Fat distributes flavor: When it is removed, the flavor must be heightened. Tomato paste, for example, not only thickens a sauce but also adds intense flavor, and a subtle sweet note. And when eggs are used, the proportion of whites (fat-free) to yolks (high in fat) is increased to reduce the fat, but the essential egg flavor is preserved.

THE FOOD PYRAMID

Creating a tempting entrée that derives less than 30 percent of its calories from fat can often be difficult. But if you include grains and vegetables in the recipe, you can begin to approach an ideal balance of food groups as currently recommended by the United States Department of Agriculture.

The USDA has defined a "Food Pyramid," a graphic guide that lists the proportions of foods required for a healthy diet. The Food Pyramid states that grains—which include bread, rice, and pasta—should make up close to half of what we consume each day; followed closely by vegetables and fruits; then meats, eggs, and dairy, and, in the smallest proportion, sweets and fats.

In creating one-pot recipes, we have respected this pyramid. The meat portions have been limited to three ounces or less, and we've used generous amounts of grains, vegetables, and fruits. We have also created a number of meatless dishes that pair beans or legumes with pasta or rice to provide a complete protein.

There are also a few treats: a bit of Canadian bacon or a creamy cheese sauce. Thus, we've orchestrated healthful meals that are a balance of color, texture, taste, and even the dictates of science.

PACKET COOKING

Cooking food "en papillote," in paper packets, is the quintessential low-fat cooking technique. Minimal fat, if any, is needed since the ingredients, sealed tightly in the paper, steam in their own juices, mingling flavors.

Classically the packets are made with parchment paper, a grease- and moisture-resistant paper that can withstand oven temperatures. The paper also makes a dramatic presentation at the table, as each diner cuts into the packet, releasing the tantalizing aromas and revealing the succulent ingredients nestled inside. Foil may be substituted for the paper, but it is less attractive, and the foil may react with especially acidic mixtures, such as tomatoes sprinkled with vinegar.

Cooking in a packet works particularly well with ingredients that cook quickly and contain some moisture: skinless, boneless chicken breasts, fish, shellfish out of their shells, vegetables, and fruits. For even cooking, be sure to cut the vegetables into small, uniform pieces so everything is done at the same time. In addition, when preheating the oven, slip in the baking sheet on which the packets will sit—this way, the packets start to cook immediately.

Cooking in Parchment

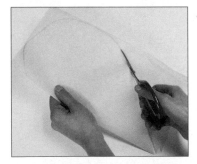

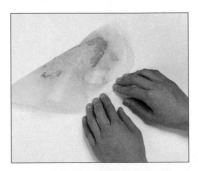

For each packet, fold a large sheet of parchment in half so the two short ends meet. Draw half a heart on the paper, using the folded seam as the center and extending the top and bottom so most of the paper is used. Cut out the heart with kitchen scissors.

Spread open the heart on a flat surface. Spoon or arrange the filling ingredients evenly along the center fold, leaving a border all around the edges. If the filling is particularly dry, first very lightly spray the paper with nonstick cooking spray to prevent sticking.

Fold one half of the heart over the filling. To seal the packet, pleat the paper edges together by folding small sections over twice, continuing around the outside until the filling is completely enclosed. Place on the preheated baking sheet and bake as the recipe directs.

SOUPS & STEWS

1

Any firm white fish will simmer well in our hearty version of the popular Mediterranean fish stew—haddock, hake, or halibut are all good stand-ins for the cod. The roasted red pepper purée, assertively laced with red pepper flakes and garlic, infuses the stew with rich, deep flavor as well as color.

BOUILLABAISSE

SERVES: 4
WORKING TIME: 25 MINUTES
TOTAL TIME: 50 MINUTES

9 thin slices (½ ounce each) French or Italian bread

1 clove garlic, halved, plus 5 cloves garlic, minced

½ cup jarred roasted red peppers, drained

¼ teaspoon red pepper flakes

1 tablespoon olive oil

1 large onion, coarsely chopped

1 cup cut fennel or celery (1-inch chunks; see tip)

⅓ cup dry white wine

⅓ cup orange juice

½ teaspoon grated orange zest

½ teaspoon fennel seeds

2 cups chopped tomatoes

¼ teaspoon salt

½ pound cod or red snapper fillets, any visible bones removed, cut into 4 pieces

½ pound sea scallops

6 ounces lump crabmeat

⅓ cup chopped fresh parsley

1. Preheat the oven to 400°. Rub the bread with the cut sides of the halved garlic clove. Reserve the garlic halves. Bake the bread for 5 to 7 minutes, or until toasted and crisp. Transfer 1 slice of the toast to a food processor or blender. Add the red peppers, red pepper flakes, reserved garlic halves, and 1 teaspoon of the oil and purée until smooth; set aside. Reserve the remaining toasts.

2. In a Dutch oven, heat the remaining 2 teaspoons oil until hot but not smoking over medium heat. Add the onion and minced garlic and cook, stirring frequently, until the onion has softened, about 7 minutes. Stir in the fennel and cook, stirring frequently, until the fennel is tender, about 5 minutes. Stir in the wine, orange juice, orange zest, and fennel seeds. Increase the heat to high, bring to a boil, and cook until the liquid has reduced by half, about 5 minutes. Stir in the tomatoes and salt and cook until the mixture is slightly thickened, about 5 minutes longer.

3. Stir in 1½ cups of water and return to a boil. Add the cod, scallops, and crabmeat, reduce the heat to medium, cover, and cook until the seafood is just opaque, about 4 minutes longer. Stir in the parsley and half of the red pepper purée. Ladle the bouillabaisse into 4 bowls. Spread the remaining red pepper purée over the reserved toasts and serve with the bouillabaisse.

Suggested accompaniment: Follow with sliced plums poached in red wine.

FAT: 6G/16%
CALORIES: 340
SATURATED FAT: .9G
CARBOHYDRATE: 33G
PROTEIN: 33G
CHOLESTEROL: 86MG
SODIUM: 647MG

TIP

To prepare fresh fennel, cut the stalks from the bulb, and trim the stem end and any tough outer sections from the bulb. Cut the bulb crosswise into 1-inch-thick slices, then cut the slices into 1-inch chunks.

Louisiana Beef Stew with Dumplings

Serves: 4
Working time: 25 minutes
Total time: 40 minutes

Mellowed with the sweetness of molasses and sharpened with ginger and red wine vinegar, this dish recalls the sultry flavors of the bayou. You can prepare the stew a day ahead and refrigerate it, but wait until reheating to prepare the dumplings—made low-fat with buttermilk—and be sure to mix with a light hand to ensure tenderness.

1¼ cups flour
½ teaspoon salt
¼ teaspoon freshly ground pepper
1 pound lean bottom round of beef, cut into ¾-inch chunks
1 tablespoon olive oil
1 large onion, cut into chunks
2 cloves garlic, minced
2 cups chopped canned no-salt-added tomatoes, with their juices
½ cup reduced-sodium chicken broth, defatted
3 tablespoons red wine vinegar
3 tablespoons molasses
½ teaspoon ground ginger
½ pound green beans, cut into 1-inch lengths
¾ teaspoon baking powder
¼ teaspoon baking soda
⅛ teaspoon nutmeg
¾ cup low-fat (1.5%) buttermilk
1 tablespoon chopped parsley

1. On a sheet of waxed paper, combine ¼ cup of the flour, ¼ teaspoon of the salt, and the pepper. Dredge the beef in the flour mixture, shaking off the excess. In a flameproof casserole or nonstick Dutch oven, heat 2 teaspoons of the oil until hot but not smoking over medium-high heat. Add the beef and cook until browned, about 4 minutes. With a slotted spoon, transfer the beef to a plate and set aside.

2. Reduce the heat to medium and add the remaining 1 teaspoon oil to the pan. Add the onion and garlic and cook, stirring frequently, until the onion has softened, about 5 minutes. Stir in the tomatoes with their juices, the broth, vinegar, molasses, and ginger. Bring to a boil, reduce to a simmer, and cook until the liquid is slightly reduced, about 5 minutes. Stir in the beans and cook for 2 minutes.

3. Meanwhile, in a medium bowl, stir together the remaining 1 cup flour, the baking powder, baking soda, remaining ¼ teaspoon salt, and nutmeg. Add the buttermilk and parsley and stir until just combined. Return the beef to the pan, stirring to blend. Return the mixture to a boil, reduce to a simmer, and drop the dumpling mixture by tablespoonfuls onto the simmering stew to make 8 dumplings. Cover and cook until the dumplings are cooked through, about 10 minutes longer.

Suggested accompaniment: Spinach salad with a lemon vinaigrette.

Fat: 11g/22%
Calories: 470
Saturated Fat: 3.2g
Carbohydrate: 58g
Protein: 34g
Cholesterol: 70mg
Sodium: 821mg

Beef Goulash

Serves: 4
Working time: 25 minutes
Total time: 40 minutes

*1¼ pounds small red potatoes,
cut into ½-inch chunks*

2 teaspoons olive oil

1 large onion, finely chopped

3 cloves garlic, minced

*2 carrots, thinly sliced on the
diagonal*

½ pound extra-lean ground beef

*6-ounce can no-salt-added
tomato paste*

½ cup dry white wine

1 tablespoon paprika

½ teaspoon caraway seeds

½ teaspoon salt

*¼ teaspoon freshly ground black
pepper*

2½ cups frozen peas, thawed

*2 tablespoons reduced-fat sour
cream*

1. In a large saucepan of boiling water, cook the potatoes until tender, about 12 minutes. Drain well and set aside.

2. Meanwhile, in a nonstick Dutch oven, heat the oil until hot but not smoking over medium heat. Add the onion and garlic and cook, stirring frequently, until the onion has softened, about 5 minutes. Stir in the carrots and cook, stirring frequently, until the carrots are tender, about 5 minutes. Add the beef and cook, stirring frequently, until no longer pink, about 4 minutes.

3. In a small bowl, combine the tomato paste, ¾ cup of water, the wine, paprika, caraway seeds, salt, and pepper and stir to blend, then stir into the pan. Bring to a boil, reduce to a simmer, cover, and cook until the beef is richly flavored, about 10 minutes.

4. Stir in the peas and potatoes, cover again, and cook just until the peas and potatoes are heated through, about 3 minutes longer. Remove from the heat, stir in the sour cream, and serve.

Suggested accompaniments: Crusty whole-wheat peasant bread, and a fresh fruit compote for dessert.

Fat: 10g/22%
Calories: 416
Saturated Fat: 3.2g
Carbohydrate: 57g
Protein: 23g
Cholesterol: 38mg
Sodium: 470mg

Chunky with vegetables, this Eastern European classic is seasoned in the traditional manner with paprika (ground mild red chili peppers) and caraway seeds. For the best flavor, use sweet Hungarian paprika, often packaged in a tin, which can range from mild to very piquant. For a final enrichment, we stir in reduced-fat sour cream, off the heat to avoid curdling.

PEPPERY FISH AND CORN CHOWDER

SERVES: 4
WORKING TIME: 20 MINUTES
TOTAL TIME: 30 MINUTES

We've used Canadian bacon here for old-fashioned flavor, and lots of vegetables. Red snapper or halibut could easily replace the cod.

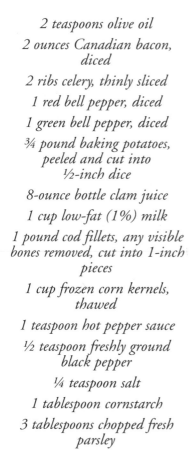

2 teaspoons olive oil

2 ounces Canadian bacon, diced

2 ribs celery, thinly sliced

1 red bell pepper, diced

1 green bell pepper, diced

¾ pound baking potatoes, peeled and cut into ½-inch dice

8-ounce bottle clam juice

1 cup low-fat (1%) milk

1 pound cod fillets, any visible bones removed, cut into 1-inch pieces

1 cup frozen corn kernels, thawed

1 teaspoon hot pepper sauce

½ teaspoon freshly ground black pepper

¼ teaspoon salt

1 tablespoon cornstarch

3 tablespoons chopped fresh parsley

1. In a Dutch oven, heat the oil until hot but not smoking over medium heat. Add the bacon and cook until lightly crisped, about 1 minute. Stir in the celery and bell peppers and cook, stirring frequently, until the vegetables are just tender, about 5 minutes.

2. Add the potatoes, stirring to coat. Add the clam juice, milk, and 1 cup of water. Bring to a boil, reduce to a simmer, cover, and cook until the potatoes are almost tender, about 7 minutes.

3. Stir in the cod, corn, hot pepper sauce, black pepper, and salt, cover again, and simmer until the cod is just opaque, about 4 minutes.

4. In a cup, combine the cornstarch and 1 tablespoon of water and stir to blend. Return the cod mixture to a boil over medium heat, stir in the cornstarch mixture, and cook, stirring constantly, until the chowder is slightly thickened, about 1 minute longer. Stir in the parsley and serve.

Suggested accompaniments: Oyster crackers, and a tossed green salad with buttermilk dressing. For the finale, blueberries garnished with lemon zest and a dollop of vanilla nonfat yogurt.

FAT: 5G/17%
CALORIES: 271
SATURATED FAT: 1.2G
CARBOHYDRATE: 28G
PROTEIN: 28G
CHOLESTEROL: 58MG
SODIUM: 606MG

Split Pea Soup with Smoked Turkey

Serves: 4
Working time: 25 minutes
Total time: 55 minutes

1 tablespoon olive oil

1 large onion, finely chopped

4 cloves garlic, minced, plus 2 cloves garlic, halved

2 carrots, thinly sliced

¾ pound sweet potatoes, peeled and thinly sliced

1 cup chopped tomato

1 cup green split peas, picked over and rinsed

¾ teaspoon dried thyme

¼ teaspoon salt

¼ teaspoon freshly ground black pepper

4 slices (1 ounce each) crusty Italian bread

6 ounces smoked turkey, cut into ½-inch dice

1 tablespoon fresh lemon juice

1. In a large pot or Dutch oven, heat the oil until hot but not smoking over medium heat. Add the onion and minced garlic and cook, stirring frequently, until the onion has softened, about 5 minutes. Stir in the carrots and sweet potatoes and cook until the carrots and potatoes are softened, about 5 minutes.

2. Add the tomato, stirring to coat. Stir in the split peas, 5 cups of water, the thyme, salt, and pepper. Bring to a boil, reduce to a simmer, and cover. Cook, stirring occasionally, until the split peas are tender, about 35 minutes.

3. Meanwhile, preheat the oven to 400°. Rub both sides of the bread with the cut sides of the halved garlic; discard the garlic. Cut the bread into 1-inch pieces for croutons. Place the bread on a baking sheet and bake for 5 minutes, or until lightly crisped. Set aside.

4. Transfer the split pea mixture to a food processor and purée until smooth, about 1 minute. Return the purée to the pot, stir in the turkey and lemon juice, and cook, uncovered, just until the turkey is heated through, about 2 minutes longer. Ladle the soup into 4 bowls, sprinkle the croutons on top, and serve.

Suggested accompaniment: Broiled cantaloupe slices dusted with some toasted ground hazelnuts.

Fat: 7g/14%
Calories: 439
Saturated Fat: 1.4g
Carbohydrate: 71g
Protein: 25g
Cholesterol: 22mg
Sodium: 765mg

*T*his all-time favorite soup gets its pleasing (and unexpected) reddish-orange color from the sweet potatoes.

*W*hether for a casual get-together or a special dinner party, this great-tasting stew, borrowed from the classic San Francisco cioppino, is a rainbow of colors and flavors. Buy the shellfish from a reliable fishmonger to guarantee absolute freshness. If good-quality fresh is not available, use canned clams (about ½ cup) and frozen shrimp.

MIXED SHELLFISH STEW

SERVES: 4
WORKING TIME: 30 MINUTES
TOTAL TIME: 55 MINUTES

1 tablespoon olive oil

⅔ cup minced shallots or red onion

5 cloves garlic, minced

1 red bell pepper, diced

¾ pound small red potatoes, quartered

½ cup chopped fresh parsley

½ cup dry white wine

½ teaspoon salt

12 littleneck or other hard-shell clams, well scrubbed (see tip)

1 pound medium shrimp, shelled and deveined

¼ cup snipped fresh chives or 2 scallions, thinly sliced

1. In a Dutch oven, heat the oil until hot but not smoking over medium heat. Add the shallots and garlic and cook, stirring frequently, until the mixture has softened, about 5 minutes. Stir in the bell pepper and cook until the pepper is crisp-tender, about 4 minutes.

2. Add the potatoes and parsley, stirring to coat. Stir in the wine, ½ cup of water, and the salt. Bring to a boil, reduce to a simmer, cover, and cook until the potatoes are almost tender, about 15 minutes.

3. Add the clams, increase the heat to medium-high, cover, and cook just until the clams have opened, about 4 minutes. Discard any clams that do not open. Stir in the shrimp, cover again, and cook until the shrimp are just opaque, about 4 minutes longer. Sprinkle the chives on top and serve.

Suggested accompaniments: Sourdough bread, and a Bibb lettuce and watercress salad with a citrus vinaigrette. Follow with Bartlett or Anjou pear halves simmered in a raspberry sugar syrup for dessert.

TIP

Before cooking, check to see that the clams are alive. Hard-shelled clams should be tightly closed or, if the shells are open, they should immediately close when lightly tapped.

FAT: 6G/19%
CALORIES: 285
SATURATED FAT: .8G
CARBOHYDRATE: 26G
PROTEIN: 27G
CHOLESTEROL: 155MG
SODIUM: 451MG

A creamy sauce coats the vegetables and moist, tender chicken in this country-kitchen specialty, perfect for a howling winter evening. The richness of this dish belies its leanness—we've removed the skin from the chicken and accented the sauce with reduced-fat sour cream. If there's no vermicelli in your pantry, use any long pasta.

COUNTRY-STYLE CHICKEN FRICASSEE

Serves: 4
Working time: 25 minutes
Total time: 40 minutes

¼ cup flour

½ teaspoon salt

¼ teaspoon freshly ground black pepper

4 whole chicken legs (about 2 pounds 2 ounces total), split and skinned (see tip)

2 teaspoons olive oil

1 large onion, finely chopped

1½ cups reduced-sodium chicken broth, defatted

1⅓ cups frozen baby lima beans or peas, thawed

1 yellow summer squash, halved lengthwise and cut into ½-inch-thick slices

6 ounces vermicelli, broken into thirds

2 tablespoons reduced-fat sour cream

2 tablespoons snipped fresh dill

1. On a sheet of waxed paper, combine the flour, ¼ teaspoon of the salt, and the pepper. Dredge the chicken in the flour mixture, shaking off the excess. In a nonstick Dutch oven, heat 1 teaspoon of the oil until hot but not smoking over medium heat. Add the chicken, in batches if necessary, and cook until lightly browned on all sides, about 6 minutes. Transfer the chicken to a plate and set aside.

2. Add the remaining 1 teaspoon oil to the pan. Add the onion and cook, stirring frequently, until the onion has softened, about 5 minutes. Stir in the broth, 1 cup of water, and the beans. Return the chicken to the pan. Bring to a boil over medium-high heat, reduce to a simmer, cover, and cook for 10 minutes.

3. Stir in the squash, vermicelli, and remaining ¼ teaspoon salt. Return to a boil, reduce to a simmer, and cover again. Cook until the vermicelli is just tender and the chicken is cooked through, about 7 minutes longer.

4. Remove from the heat and stir in the sour cream and dill. Divide the chicken fricassee among 4 bowls and serve.

Suggested accompaniments: Buttermilk biscuits, followed by baked apples stuffed with raisins and rolled oats.

Fat: 11g/18%
Calories: 525
Saturated Fat: 2.5g
Carbohydrate: 59g
Protein: 46g
Cholesterol: 134mg
Sodium: 691mg

TIP

To split a whole chicken leg, slightly stretch the drumstick and thigh apart to find the ball joint, and, with a sharp boning knife, cleanly cut through the joint. Grabbing the leg at opposite ends, pull apart the thigh and drumstick.

CUBAN-STYLE BEEF STEW

SERVES: 4
WORKING TIME: 15 MINUTES
TOTAL TIME: 20 MINUTES

*T*his quick-to-fix stew offers all the body of a long-simmered concoction, thanks to instant taste tricks—jarred salsa and canned green chilies.

2 tablespoons flour

¼ teaspoon salt

¼ teaspoon freshly ground black pepper

½ pound lean bottom round of beef, cut into 1-inch chunks

2 teaspoons olive oil

1 red bell pepper, cut into ½-inch dice

1½ cups mild or medium-hot prepared low-sodium salsa

16-ounce can black beans, rinsed and drained

4-ounce can chopped mild green chilies

½ teaspoon dried oregano

1. On a sheet of waxed paper, combine the flour, salt, and black pepper. Dredge the beef in the flour mixture, shaking off the excess. In a nonstick Dutch oven, heat the oil until hot but not smoking over medium heat. Add the beef and cook, stirring frequently, until browned, about 5 minutes. With a slotted spoon, transfer the beef to a plate and set aside.

2. Add the bell pepper to the pan and cook, stirring frequently, until the pepper is softened, about 4 minutes. Stir in the salsa, black beans, chilies, and oregano. Bring to a boil, reduce to a simmer, cover, and cook until the flavors have blended, about 5 minutes.

3. Return the beef to the pan and cook, uncovered, until the beef is just cooked through, about 5 minutes longer. Ladle the stew into 4 bowls and serve.

Suggested accompaniments: Romaine and shredded carrot salad with a red wine vinaigrette. For dessert, broiled sliced papaya sprinkled with brown sugar and vanilla.

FAT: 6G/24%
CALORIES: 229
SATURATED FAT: 1.4G
CARBOHYDRATE: 24G
PROTEIN: 19G
CHOLESTEROL: 33MG
SODIUM: 548MG

BEEF AND BARLEY SOUP

SERVES: 4
WORKING TIME: 20 MINUTES
TOTAL TIME: 50 MINUTES

2 teaspoons olive oil

1 large onion, coarsely chopped

3 cloves garlic, minced

2 carrots, thinly sliced

2 turnips, diced

2 leeks (white and light green parts only), diced

½ cup pearl barley

2 cups reduced-sodium beef broth, defatted

½ teaspoon dried thyme

½ teaspoon freshly ground black pepper

¼ teaspoon salt

6 ounces lean bottom round of beef, cut into ½-inch pieces

1 tablespoon fresh lemon juice

3 tablespoons chopped fresh parsley

1 teaspoon grated lemon zest

1. In a nonstick Dutch oven, heat the oil until hot but not smoking over low heat. Add the onion and garlic and cook, stirring frequently, until the onion has softened, about 5 minutes.

2. Add the carrots, turnips, leeks, and barley, stirring to coat. Stir in the broth, 3 cups of water, the thyme, pepper, and salt and increase the heat to high. Bring to a boil, reduce to a simmer, cover, and cook until the barley and vegetables are tender, about 30 minutes.

3. Stir in the beef, cover again, and simmer until the beef is cooked through, about 5 minutes longer. Remove from the heat and stir in the lemon juice. Ladle the soup into 4 bowls, sprinkle the parsley and lemon zest on top, and serve.

Suggested accompaniments: Semolina bread, a roasted red pepper salad with an herb vinaigrette and, for dessert, orange sections and dried cranberries splashed with cranberry liqueur.

FAT: 5G/17%
CALORIES: 271
SATURATED FAT: 1.2G
CARBOHYDRATE: 42G
PROTEIN: 16G
CHOLESTEROL: 25MG
SODIUM: 542MG

O*ur savory winter warmer, chock-full of root vegetables, has a touch of lemon that sets it apart from the usual.*

PORK AND THREE-PEPPER STEW

SERVES: 4
WORKING TIME: 25 MINUTES
TOTAL TIME: 40 MINUTES

6 ounces orzo

2 tablespoons flour

½ teaspoon salt

¼ teaspoon freshly ground black
pepper

½ pound lean boneless pork loin,
cut into 1-inch chunks

2 teaspoons olive oil

1 red bell pepper, diced

1 green bell pepper, diced

1 yellow bell pepper, diced

1 medium red onion, halved
and thinly sliced

3 tablespoons balsamic vinegar

2 teaspoons firmly packed dark
brown sugar

1½ cups reduced-sodium chicken
broth, defatted

2 tablespoons chopped fresh
parsley

1. In a large saucepan of boiling water, cook the orzo until just tender. Drain well. Set aside.

2. Meanwhile, on a sheet of waxed paper, combine the flour, ¼ teaspoon of the salt, and the black pepper. Dredge the pork in the flour mixture, shaking off the excess. Spray a Dutch oven with nonstick cooking spray, add the oil, and heat until hot but not smoking over medium heat. Add the pork and cook, stirring frequently, until golden brown, about 4 minutes. With a slotted spoon, transfer the pork to a plate and set aside.

3. Add the bell peppers and onion to the pan, stirring to coat. Stir in ⅓ cup of water, cover, and cook, stirring occasionally, until the peppers and onions are tender, about 7 minutes.

4. Stir in the vinegar and brown sugar and cook, uncovered, for 1 minute. Add the broth and remaining ¼ teaspoon salt, bring to a boil, reduce to a simmer, and stir in the orzo. Return the pork to the pan, cover again, and cook until the pork is cooked through and the orzo is creamy, about 3 minutes longer. Sprinkle with the parsley and serve.

Suggested accompaniments: Sesame bread sticks, and a dessert of broiled banana slices topped with mango nonfat yogurt.

FAT: 6G/17%
CALORIES: 323
SATURATED FAT: 1.5G
CARBOHYDRATE: 45G
PROTEIN: 21G
CHOLESTEROL: 33MG
SODIUM: 556MG

For this simple stew, tender lean pork is deliciously accented by a sweet-and-sour broth—the tang of balsamic vinegar balanced with a hint of brown sugar. For a creamy texture, we've added a handful of orzo. If you don't have a nonstick pot, create your own by coating a regular pan with nonstick cooking spray so that you can sauté in a minimum of oil.

CHICKEN AND MUSHROOM STEW

*T*he dark meat from the chicken thighs, robustly enhanced with tarragon, makes this knife-and-fork stew especially rich. Simmering the garlic cloves mellows their usual sharpness, while shallots—the most mildly flavored of all the onions—add subtle sweetness and body. As is true of many stews, this one is excellent prepared a day ahead so the flavors can meld.

2 tablespoons flour
½ teaspoon salt
½ teaspoon freshly ground black pepper
10 ounces skinless, boneless chicken thighs, cut into 1-inch chunks
2 teaspoons olive oil
8 shallots, peeled
8 cloves garlic, peeled
¾ pound small red potatoes, cut into ½-inch chunks
¾ pound mushrooms, quartered
2 carrots, thinly sliced
¾ cup reduced-sodium chicken broth, defatted
2 tablespoons fresh lemon juice
1 teaspoon dried tarragon
1¼ cups frozen peas
3 scallions, halved lengthwise and cut into 1-inch lengths
¼ cup chopped fresh parsley

1. On a sheet of waxed paper, combine the flour, ¼ teaspoon of the salt, and ¼ teaspoon of the pepper. Dredge the chicken in the flour mixture, shaking off the excess. Spray a large saucepan or Dutch oven with nonstick cooking spray, add the oil, and heat until hot but not smoking over medium heat. Add the chicken and cook, stirring frequently, until lightly browned, about 5 minutes. With a slotted spoon, transfer the chicken to a plate and set aside.

2. Add the shallots and garlic to the pan and cook, shaking the pan frequently, until the mixture is lightly golden, about 2 minutes. Add the potatoes, mushrooms, and carrots, stirring to coat. Stir in the broth, lemon juice, tarragon, remaining ¼ teaspoon salt, and remaining ¼ teaspoon pepper. Bring to a boil, reduce to a simmer, cover, and cook until the potatoes and carrots are tender, about 15 minutes.

3. Return the chicken to the pan along with the peas and scallions and stir well to combine. Simmer, uncovered, until the chicken is cooked through and the peas are hot, about 3 minutes longer. Stir in the parsley and serve.

Suggested accompaniment: Angel food cake with a scoop of strawberry ice milk.

FAT: 6G/18%
CALORIES: 292
SATURATED FAT: 1.1G
CARBOHYDRATE: 39G
PROTEIN: 22G
CHOLESTEROL: 59MG
SODIUM: 535MG

CURRIED PORK STEW

SERVES: 4
WORKING TIME: 20 MINUTES
TOTAL TIME: 45 MINUTES

Rather than using a store-bought curry powder, we've boosted the flavor of this stew by creating our own with a variety of "sweet" spices.

2 tablespoons flour

½ teaspoon salt

¼ teaspoon freshly ground black pepper

½ pound lean boneless pork loin, cut into 1-inch chunks

2 teaspoons olive oil

¾ teaspoon ground cumin

½ teaspoon ground coriander

½ teaspoon ground ginger

½ teaspoon turmeric

2½ cups cauliflower florets

¾ pound small red potatoes, cut into ½-inch chunks

1 Granny Smith apple, cored and diced

¾ cup chopped canned no-salt-added tomatoes, with their juices

¼ cup plain low-fat yogurt

3 tablespoons chopped fresh cilantro or parsley

1. On a sheet of waxed paper, combine the flour, ¼ teaspoon of the salt, and the pepper. Dredge the pork in the flour mixture, shaking off the excess. Reserve the remaining flour mixture. In a nonstick Dutch oven, heat the oil until hot but not smoking over medium heat. Add the pork and cook, stirring frequently, until browned, about 5 minutes. With a slotted spoon, transfer the pork to a plate and set aside.

2. Add the cumin, coriander, ginger, and turmeric to the pan and cook, stirring constantly, until fragrant, about 10 seconds. Stir in the cauliflower, potatoes, and apple. Add the tomatoes with their juices, ½ cup of water, and the remaining ¼ teaspoon salt. Bring to a boil, reduce to a simmer, cover, and cook until the cauliflower and potatoes are almost tender, 15 to 20 minutes.

3. In a small bowl, combine the reserved flour mixture and the yogurt and stir to blend, then stir into the simmering vegetable mixture until well combined. Return the pork to the pan, add the cilantro, and cook, uncovered, until the pork is cooked through and the vegetables are tender, about 5 minutes longer. Ladle the stew into 4 bowls and serve.

Suggested accompaniments: Toasted pita bread wedges and, to finish, stewed apricots sprinkled with toasted almonds.

FAT: 6G/22%
CALORIES: 241
SATURATED FAT: 1.6G
CARBOHYDRATE: 30G
PROTEIN: 17G
CHOLESTEROL: 34MG
SODIUM: 336MG

Moroccan Chicken Stew with Lemon

Serves: 4
Working time: 20 minutes
Total time: 40 minutes

4 cloves garlic, minced

1 cup sliced scallions

3 tablespoons fresh lemon juice

¾ teaspoon ground cumin

⅛ teaspoon ground allspice

¾ pound skinless, boneless chicken breasts, cut into 2-inch chunks

1 tablespoon olive oil

2 cups peeled, seeded, and cut butternut squash (1½-inch chunks)

1 medium red onion, diced

1 cup canned chick-peas, rinsed and drained

⅔ cup reduced-sodium chicken broth, defatted

¼ cup chopped fresh parsley

2 teaspoons cornstarch

¼ cup chopped pitted green olives (optional)

1. In a large bowl, combine the garlic, ½ cup of the scallions, the lemon juice, cumin, and allspice and stir to blend. Add the chicken and toss until well coated. Cover with plastic wrap and refrigerate for 20 to 30 minutes.

2. Meanwhile, in a Dutch oven, heat the oil until hot but not smoking over medium heat. Add the squash and onion and cook, stirring frequently, until the squash and onion are lightly golden, about 5 minutes.

3. Stir in the chick-peas, broth, and parsley and bring to a boil. Add the chicken with its marinade, reduce to a simmer, cover, and cook until the vegetables are tender and the chicken is cooked through, about 8 minutes.

4. In a cup, combine the cornstarch and 1 tablespoon of water and stir to blend. Stir the olives, remaining ½ cup scallions, and the cornstarch mixture into the simmering stew, increase the heat to medium-high, and bring to a boil. Cook, stirring constantly, until the stew is slightly thickened, about 1 minute longer. Spoon the stew into 4 bowls and serve.

Suggested accompaniments: Herbal tea, and green and red seedless grapes with goat cheese rounds for dessert.

Fat: 6g/22%
Calories: 248
Saturated Fat: .8g
Carbohydrate: 25g
Protein: 25g
Cholesterol: 49mg
Sodium: 258mg

Sweet butternut squash colorfully complements this chicken, while cumin and allspice lend a lovely fragrance.

QUICK BEEF CHILI

SERVES: 4
WORKING TIME: 25 MINUTES
TOTAL TIME: 35 MINUTES

1 teaspoon olive oil

1 large onion, finely chopped

1 green bell pepper, cut into ¾-inch dice

3 cloves garlic, minced

¾ pound extra-lean ground beef

1 tablespoon plus 1 teaspoon mild chili powder

2 teaspoons flour

1 teaspoon ground cumin

¾ teaspoon ground coriander

¾ teaspoon dried oregano

Two 14½-ounce cans no-salt-added stewed tomatoes, chopped with their juices

2 tablespoons no-salt-added tomato paste

½ teaspoon salt

Two 16-ounce cans red kidney beans, rinsed and drained

1¾ cups frozen corn kernels

1. In a Dutch oven, heat the oil until hot but not smoking over medium heat. Add the onion, bell pepper, and garlic and cook, stirring frequently, until the vegetables are fragrant and softened, about 7 minutes.

2. Add the beef and cook, stirring frequently, until no longer pink, about 4 minutes. Stir in the chili powder, flour, cumin, coriander, and oregano until well combined. Stir in the tomatoes with their juices, the tomato paste, and salt and cook, stirring frequently, until the beef is nicely coated and the mixture is slightly thickened, 5 to 7 minutes.

3. Stir in the beans and corn and cook until the vegetables are heated through, about 2 minutes longer.

Suggested accompaniments: Small squares of corn bread, coleslaw made with nonfat mayonnaise, and reduced-fat chocolate chip cookies.

For an extra zippy chili, we've enhanced the usual chili powder seasoning with cumin, coriander, and oregano. To keep the sodium within reason, we've used no-salt-added tomato products and rinsed the beans. Make the chili a day ahead for even better flavor.

FAT: 12G/23%
CALORIES: 484
SATURATED FAT: 3.8G
CARBOHYDRATE: 65G
PROTEIN: 35G
CHOLESTEROL: 53MG
SODIUM: 688MG

I_n our rendition of the time-honored hearty combination of beans and pasta, we've doubled up on the green: kale and cabbage, perfect for adding flavor and body to soups, and high in health-promoting beta carotene and vitamin C. If reheating leftovers, add a little chicken broth or water since pasta absorbs liquid as it stands.

Italian Pasta-Vegetable Soup

SERVES: 4
WORKING TIME: 25 MINUTES
TOTAL TIME: 40 MINUTES

1 tablespoon olive oil

1 large onion, coarsely chopped

3 cloves garlic, minced

2 carrots, halved lengthwise and cut into thin slices

5 cups ¼-inch-wide shredded kale (see tip) or spinach

2 cups chopped cabbage

2 cups reduced-sodium chicken broth, defatted

5.5-ounce can reduced-sodium tomato-vegetable juice

16-ounce can red kidney beans, rinsed and drained

5 ounces small elbow macaroni

½ teaspoon salt

¼ cup grated Parmesan cheese

1. In a large saucepan or Dutch oven, heat the oil until hot but not smoking over medium heat. Add the onion and garlic and cook, stirring frequently, until the onion has softened, about 5 minutes.

2. Stir in the carrots, kale, and cabbage and cook, stirring frequently, until the vegetables have softened, about 4 minutes. Stir in the broth, tomato-vegetable juice, and 3 cups of water. Bring to a boil, reduce to a simmer, cover, and cook until the flavors have blended, about 5 minutes.

3. Uncover the soup, return to a boil over medium heat, and stir in the beans, macaroni, and salt. Cook, uncovered, until the macaroni is tender, about 8 minutes longer.

4. Remove from the heat and stir in 1 tablespoon of the Parmesan. Serve the soup with the remaining 3 tablespoons Parmesan sprinkled on top.

Suggested accompaniments: Italian or French bread. Finish with espresso and amaretti cookies.

FAT: 7G/17%
CALORIES: 373
SATURATED FAT: 1.6G
CARBOHYDRATE: 61G
PROTEIN: 19G
CHOLESTEROL: 4MG
SODIUM: 945MG

TIP

To prepare kale for cooking, rinse well, then separate the individual leaves. Working with one leaf at a time, pinch off or cut the tough, inedible stems and discard. Cut the leaves into ¼-inch-wide shreds.

Coq au Vin

SERVES: 4
WORKING TIME: 25 MINUTES
TOTAL TIME: 50 MINUTES

Deeply flavored with red wine and brandy, this saucy French-style classic captures the very goodness of simple home cooking.

3 tablespoons flour

½ teaspoon salt

¼ teaspoon freshly ground black pepper

4 bone-in chicken thighs (about 1 pound 6 ounces total), skinned

2 teaspoons olive oil

¾ pound small red potatoes, cut into ½-inch chunks

2 carrots, halved lengthwise and cut into 1-inch-thick slices

½ cup frozen pearl onions, thawed

½ pound mushrooms, quartered

2 tablespoons brandy

½ cup dry red wine

½ cup reduced-sodium chicken broth, defatted

¾ teaspoon dried tarragon

½ teaspoon dried rosemary

3 scallions, halved lengthwise and cut into 1½-inch lengths

1. On a sheet of waxed paper, combine the flour, ¼ teaspoon of the salt, and the pepper. Dredge the chicken in the flour mixture, shaking off the excess. In a nonstick Dutch oven, heat the oil until hot but not smoking over medium heat. Add the chicken and cook until lightly browned, about 5 minutes. Transfer the chicken to a plate and set aside.

2. Add the potatoes, carrots, and onions to the pan and cook, shaking the pan frequently, until the vegetables are lightly browned, about 5 minutes. Add the mushrooms, stirring to coat. Add the brandy and cook until the liquid has evaporated, about 3 minutes.

3. Add the wine, increase the heat to medium-high, bring to a boil, and cook for 1 minute. Stir in the broth, tarragon, rosemary, and remaining ¼ teaspoon salt. Return the chicken to the pan. Return the mixture to a boil, reduce to a simmer, cover, and cook until the chicken is cooked through and the vegetables are tender, about 25 minutes.

4. Stir in the scallions and cook until the scallions are slightly softened, about 1 minute longer. Divide the chicken mixture among 4 bowls and serve.

Suggested accompaniments: Sparkling apple cider, and a shredded beet salad with a Dijon mustard vinaigrette.

FAT: 7G/20%
CALORIES: 310
SATURATED FAT: 1.5G
CARBOHYDRATE: 30G
PROTEIN: 27G
CHOLESTEROL: 93MG
SODIUM: 478MG

SKILLET DINNERS
2

Seafood-Sausage Paella

Serves: 4
Working time: 35 minutes
Total time: 1 hour

2 teaspoons olive oil

2 ounces Virginia ham, cut into matchsticks

1 large onion, cut into 1-inch chunks

1 red bell pepper, cut into 1-inch squares

2 ounces hot turkey sausage, thinly sliced

1 cup long-grain rice

1 cup reduced-sodium chicken broth, defatted

½ teaspoon dried thyme

½ teaspoon freshly ground black pepper

½ teaspoon turmeric

¼ teaspoon red pepper flakes

1 pound plum tomatoes (about 4), diced

½ pound large shrimp, shelled and deveined

6 ounces swordfish steak, cut into 1-inch chunks

1 cup frozen peas, thawed

1. In a large skillet, heat the oil until hot but not smoking over medium heat. Add the ham and cook until lightly crisped, about 4 minutes. Add the onion and cook, stirring frequently, until the onion is softened and lightly golden, about 7 minutes.

2. Add the bell pepper and cook, stirring frequently, until the pepper is softened, about 5 minutes. Stir in the turkey sausage and cook until no longer pink, about 4 minutes. Add the rice, stirring to coat. Stir in the broth, 1 cup of water, the thyme, black pepper, turmeric, and red pepper flakes. Bring to a boil, reduce to a simmer, cover, and cook until the rice is tender, about 17 minutes.

3. Stir in the tomatoes, shrimp, and swordfish. Cover again and cook until the shrimp and swordfish are just opaque, about 5 minutes. Add the peas, cover again, and cook until the peas are just heated through, about 1 minute longer.

Suggested accompaniments: Mixed green salad with a sherry wine vinaigrette. For dessert, reduced-calorie lemon pudding garnished with crumbled gingersnaps.

Fat: 8g/17%
Calories: 422
Saturated Fat: 2.1g
Carbohydrate: 54g
Protein: 31g
Cholesterol: 104mg
Sodium: 623mg

This popular rice dish with Spanish origins is colored a vivid yellow from turmeric rather than the traditional, but outrageously expensive, saffron. Our low-fat tricks here are lean turkey sausage and just a little Virginia ham for flavoring. Substitute tuna or salmon for the swordfish, if you like, and double the recipe for a spectacular buffet dish for a crowd.

CHICKEN-FRIED STEAK DINNER

SERVES: 4
WORKING TIME: 35 MINUTES
TOTAL TIME: 1 HOUR

A*s* tasty as their classic Texas inspiration, these crispy, cheese-topped steaks are irresistible served hot from the skillet.

12 ounces Italian bread, halved lengthwise and then crosswise (4 pieces)

2 cloves garlic, halved

2 egg whites

⅓ cup grated Parmesan cheese

⅓ cup plain dried bread crumbs

½ pound top round of beef, cut into four ¼-inch-thick steaks

1 tablespoon olive oil

1 medium red onion, halved and thinly sliced

1 red bell pepper, thinly sliced

¼ pound mushrooms, thinly sliced

Two 8-ounce cans no-salt-added tomato sauce

¼ cup chopped fresh basil

2 ounces part-skim mozzarella cheese, shredded (about ½ cup)

1. Preheat the oven to 400°. Rub the bread with the cut sides of the garlic; discard the garlic. Bake the bread for 5 to 7 minutes, or until toasted. Place the toasts on 4 serving plates and set aside.

2. Meanwhile, in a shallow dish, lightly beat the egg whites and 1 tablespoon of water. On a sheet of waxed paper, spread the Parmesan. On a plate, spread the bread crumbs. Dredge the steaks in the Parmesan, pressing to adhere. Dip the steaks into the egg whites, then into the bread crumbs, turning to coat.

3. Spray a large nonstick skillet with nonstick cooking spray, add the oil, and heat until hot but not smoking over medium-high heat. Add the steaks and cook until golden brown and crisp, about 2 minutes per side. Transfer the steaks to a plate. Set aside.

4. Add the onion and bell pepper to the pan, reduce the heat to medium, and cook, stirring frequently, until lightly golden, about 5 minutes. Add the mushrooms and cook until tender, about 5 minutes. Stir in the tomato sauce and basil, cover, and cook until slightly thickened, about 5 minutes. Return the steaks to the pan, spoon the sauce over, and sprinkle the mozzarella on top. Cover again and cook until the cheese is melted, about 1 minute. Divide the steaks, sauce, and vegetables among the toasts and serve.

Suggested accompaniments: Cherry tomatoes, and reduced-fat brownies.

FAT: 14G/24%
CALORIES: 517
SATURATED FAT: 4.6G
CARBOHYDRATE: 66G
PROTEIN: 33G
CHOLESTEROL: 46MG
SODIUM: 850MG

COUSCOUS WITH CHICKEN AND VEGETABLES

SERVES: 4
WORKING TIME: 20 MINUTES
TOTAL TIME: 35 MINUTES

2 teaspoons olive oil

1 large onion, diced

4 cloves garlic, minced

2 carrots, cut into ½-inch-thick slices

6 ounces skinless, boneless chicken thighs, cut into ½-inch chunks

1 teaspoon curry powder

½ teaspoon ground ginger

¼ teaspoon cinnamon

¼ teaspoon salt

⅛ teaspoon cayenne pepper

⅛ teaspoon ground allspice

⅛ teaspoon freshly ground black pepper

1 yellow summer squash, halved lengthwise and cut into ½-inch-thick slices

1 zucchini, halved lengthwise and cut into ½-inch-thick slices

1 cup reduced-sodium chicken broth, defatted

⅔ cup couscous

¼ cup chopped fresh cilantro

1. In a large nonstick skillet, heat the oil until hot but not smoking over medium heat. Add the onion and garlic and cook, stirring frequently, until the onion is softened, about 7 minutes.

2. Stir in the carrots and cook, stirring frequently, until the carrots are well coated, about 2 minutes. Add the chicken and cook, stirring frequently, until the chicken is no longer pink, about 2 minutes. Stir in the curry powder, ginger, cinnamon, salt, cayenne, allspice, and black pepper and cook, stirring constantly, until the mixture is fragrant, about 1 minute.

3. Stir in the yellow squash, zucchini, broth, and ½ cup of water and bring to a boil. Add the couscous and cook, stirring frequently, until the liquid is absorbed and the chicken is cooked through, about 5 minutes longer. Stir in the cilantro and serve.

Suggested accompaniments: Sesame flat breads, sliced cucumbers with an herbed yogurt dressing, and blood oranges or nectarines for dessert.

FAT: 4G/14%
CALORIES: 250
SATURATED FAT: .8G
CARBOHYDRATE: 37G
PROTEIN: 15G
CHOLESTEROL: 35MG
SODIUM: 353MG

This simple dish—which is a snap to prepare—will fill the kitchen with the aroma of sweet spices.

Skillet Antipasto Dinner

Serves: 4
Working time: 25 minutes
Total time: 40 minutes

After the vegetables are prepped, this riotously colorful dish is nothing more than a quick stir-fry. Frozen artichoke hearts are immeasurably easier to prepare than fresh ones, and when mixed with other ingredients, they're just as tasty. You may try this dish with ham or smoked chicken, and substitute red wine vinegar for the balsamic.

¾ pound small red potatoes, quartered

9-ounce package frozen artichoke hearts

1 tablespoon extra-virgin olive oil

1 medium red onion, cut into 1-inch chunks

1 red bell pepper, cut into 1-inch pieces

2 ribs celery, halved lengthwise and cut into 1-inch slices

1 zucchini, cut into 1-by-½-inch strips

1¼ cups canned chick-peas, rinsed and drained

¼ pound smoked turkey, cut into 1½-by-½-inch strips

3 tablespoons balsamic vinegar

1 tablespoon chopped fresh parsley

1. In a large saucepan of boiling water, cook the potatoes for 10 minutes. Add the artichokes and continue to cook until the potatoes are just tender, about 5 minutes longer. Drain the potatoes and artichokes well and pat dry with paper towels. Set aside.

2. In a large nonstick skillet, heat 2 teaspoons of the oil until hot but not smoking over medium heat. Add the onion and bell pepper and cook, stirring frequently, until the pepper is crisp-tender, about 5 minutes. Stir in the potatoes and artichokes and cook, stirring frequently, until the artichokes are tender, about 5 minutes.

3. Stir in the celery and zucchini and cook, stirring frequently, until the celery and zucchini are crisp-tender, about 3 minutes. Stir in the chick-peas and turkey and cook just until the chick-peas and turkey are heated through, about 3 minutes longer.

4. Gently stir in the remaining 1 teaspoon oil, the vinegar, and parsley. Spoon the antipasto mixture onto 4 plates and serve.

Suggested accompaniments: Italian bread, romaine and endive salad with a sun-dried tomato vinaigrette, and frozen grapes to finish.

Fat: 6g/22%
Calories: 250
Saturated Fat: 1g
Carbohydrate: 37g
Protein: 14g
Cholesterol: 15mg
Sodium: 449mg

STIR-FRIED BEEF AND VEGETABLES WITH ORZO

SERVES: 4
WORKING TIME: 25 MINUTES
TOTAL TIME: 35 MINUTES

1¼ cups orzo

2 tablespoons flour

10 ounces lean bottom round of beef, cut into 1½-by-¼-inch strips

2 teaspoons dark Oriental sesame oil

½ pound mushrooms, quartered

1 carrot, cut into matchsticks

3 cloves garlic, minced

1 tablespoon minced fresh ginger

3 cups diced Napa cabbage

1 cup halved cherry tomatoes

½ cup reduced-sodium beef broth, defatted

2 tablespoons reduced-sodium soy sauce

¼ teaspoon firmly packed brown sugar

¼ teaspoon red pepper flakes

2 teaspoons cornstarch

1. In a large saucepan of boiling water, cook the orzo until just tender. Drain well and set aside.

2. Meanwhile, on a sheet of waxed paper, spread the flour. Dredge the beef in the flour, shaking off the excess. In a large nonstick wok or skillet, heat the oil until hot but not smoking over medium heat. Add the beef and cook, stirring frequently, until browned, about 4 minutes. With a slotted spoon, transfer the beef to a plate and set aside.

3. Add the mushrooms, carrot, garlic, and ginger to the pan, stirring to coat. Cook, stirring frequently, until the carrot is crisp-tender, about 4 minutes. Stir in the cabbage, cherry tomatoes, broth, soy sauce, brown sugar, and red pepper flakes. Increase the heat to medium-high and bring to a boil.

4. In a cup, combine the cornstarch and 1 tablespoon of water, stir to blend, and stir into the boiling vegetable mixture along with the orzo. Cook, stirring constantly, until the mixture is slightly thickened, about 2 minutes. Return the beef to the pan and cook until the beef is heated through, about 1 minute longer.

Suggested accompaniment: Peach halves drizzled with honey and broiled, then dusted with toasted chopped macadamia nuts.

FAT: 8G/17%
CALORIES: 422
SATURATED FAT: 1.9G
CARBOHYDRATE: 61G
PROTEIN: 27G
CHOLESTEROL: 42MG
SODIUM: 442MG

Here orzo, a rice-shaped pasta often found in Greek cooking, absorbs the Asian flavors of the nutty dark sesame oil and fragrant ginger—fusion cooking at its best. If Napa cabbage, mild-tasting with light green crinkly leaves, is unavailable, substitute romaine lettuce. And for an even deeper flavor, replace the regular button mushrooms with fresh shiitakes.

*C*ooling slices of cucumber temper fiery black and cayenne pepper and pungent fresh ginger, and the large, meaty shrimp soak up all the different flavors. To lightly thicken the sauce, we've used the classic stir-fry method, mixing cornstarch with water and stirring it in for the final step. Avoid overcooking or the cornstarch will lose its thickening power.

44

Hot and Tangy Shrimp

Serves: 4
Working time: 25 minutes
Total time: 40 minutes

½ teaspoon freshly ground black pepper

½ teaspoon ground ginger

½ teaspoon salt

⅛ teaspoon ground allspice

⅛ teaspoon cayenne pepper

1½ pounds large shrimp, shelled and deveined

2 teaspoons olive oil

½ cup minced scallions

4 cloves garlic, slivered

1 tablespoon minced fresh ginger

¾ pound sweet potatoes, peeled and cut into ½-inch dice

1 red bell pepper, cut into ½-inch dice

1 cup reduced-sodium chicken broth, defatted

1 cucumber, peeled, halved lengthwise, seeded, and cut into ½-inch-thick slices (see tip)

2 teaspoons cornstarch

2 tablespoons fresh lime juice

1. In a large bowl, combine the black pepper, ground ginger, salt, allspice, and cayenne and stir to blend. Add the shrimp, rubbing in the spices until well coated. Set aside.

2. Spray a large nonstick skillet with nonstick cooking spray, add the oil, and heat until hot but not smoking over medium heat. Add the scallions, garlic, and fresh ginger and cook, stirring frequently, until the mixture is fragrant, about 2 minutes. Stir in the sweet potatoes and bell pepper and cook, stirring frequently, until the pepper is crisp-tender, about 4 minutes.

3. Stir in the broth and bring to a boil. Reduce to a simmer, cover, and cook until the sweet potatoes are tender, about 10 minutes. Stir in the cucumber and shrimp, cover again, and cook until the shrimp are almost opaque, about 3 minutes.

4. In a cup, combine the cornstarch and 1 tablespoon of water and stir to blend. Bring the shrimp mixture to a boil over medium-high heat, stir in the cornstarch mixture along with the lime juice, and cook, stirring constantly, until the mixture is slightly thickened and the shrimp are just opaque, about 1 minute longer. Spoon the shrimp and vegetables onto a platter and serve.

Suggested accompaniment: Fat-free toasted pound cake slices topped with mandarin orange sections marinated in Marsala wine.

Fat: 5g/17%
Calories: 268
Saturated Fat: .8g
Carbohydrate: 24g
Protein: 31g
Cholesterol: 210mg
Sodium: 654mg

TIP

To remove the seeds from a cucumber, first cut the peeled cucumber in half lengthwise. Holding a half in one hand, scoop out the seeds with a spoon, leaving the cucumber shell intact.

PORK "UN-FRIED" RICE

SERVES: 4
WORKING TIME: 30 MINUTES
TOTAL TIME: 45 MINUTES

This vivid potpourri retains all the textures and colors of the usual fried rice, but without the extra fat and calories. We've used a mere two teaspoons of oil for "frying" before gently simmering the ingredients, thus fusing the flavors. Strips of beef top round or chicken breast would be equally delicious in place of the pork.

2 teaspoons vegetable oil

4 scallions (white and tender green parts only), thinly sliced

3 cloves garlic, minced

1 tablespoon minced fresh ginger

1 cup long-grain rice

1⅓ cups reduced-sodium chicken broth, defatted

½ pound lean boneless pork loin, cut into 1½-by-¼-inch strips

⅔ cup ¼-inch-wide shredded Napa cabbage

1 red bell pepper, diced

½ pound snow peas, trimmed and cut diagonally in half

1 cup frozen peas, thawed

1 tablespoon reduced-sodium soy sauce

1 tablespoon cider vinegar

1. In a large skillet, heat the oil until hot but not smoking over medium heat. Add the scallions, garlic, and ginger and cook, stirring frequently, until the mixture is softened, about 3 minutes. Add the rice, stirring to coat. Add the broth and 1 cup of water, bring to a boil, reduce to a simmer, cover, and cook until the rice is tender, about 15 minutes.

2. Stir in the pork, cabbage, bell pepper, and snow peas. Cover again and cook, stirring frequently, until the cabbage and pepper are just crisp-tender and the pork is almost cooked through, about 5 minutes.

3. Stir in the peas, soy sauce, and vinegar and cook, uncovered, stirring constantly, until the pork is cooked through and the rice is lightly golden, about 5 minutes longer.

Suggested accompaniments: Almond or oolong tea, fortune cookies, and fresh cherries steeped in red wine.

FAT: 6G/16%
CALORIES: 346
SATURATED FAT: 1.5G
CARBOHYDRATE: 51G
PROTEIN: 21G
CHOLESTEROL: 33MG
SODIUM: 443MG

HAM AND SWEET POTATO SAUTÉ

SERVES: 4
WORKING TIME: 20 MINUTES
TOTAL TIME: 30 MINUTES

This homey weeknight supper is enlivened with mango chutney and Dijon mustard, and for a hint of delicate sweetness and texture, we've slipped in wedges of Bartlett pears. If you'd like, press your microwave oven into service for preparing the sweet potatoes: Cook, covered, in a microwave-safe casserole on high power for four to five minutes.

1 pound sweet potatoes, peeled and cut into 1-inch chunks

2 teaspoons olive oil

¾ cup diced onion

2 Bartlett pears, peeled, cored, and cut into 8 wedges each

3 tablespoons chopped mango chutney

1 tablespoon fresh lemon juice

2 teaspoons Dijon mustard

3 cups broccoli florets

½ pound boneless ham steak, cut into 1-inch chunks

1. In a large saucepan of boiling water, cook the sweet potatoes until almost tender, about 5 minutes. Drain well and set aside.

2. Meanwhile, in a large nonstick skillet, heat the oil until hot but not smoking over medium heat. Add the onion and cook, stirring frequently, until the onion is lightly browned, about 5 minutes.

3. Add the pears to the skillet, stirring to coat. Stir in the chutney, ¼ cup of water, the lemon juice, and mustard. Bring to a boil, reduce to a simmer, cover, and cook until the pears are almost tender, about 5 minutes (cooking time will vary depending on the ripeness of the pears).

4. Stir in the sweet potatoes and broccoli and cook, uncovered, until the broccoli is tender, about 5 minutes. Stir in the ham and cook until the ham is just heated through, about 4 minutes longer.

Suggested accompaniments: Escarole salad with a parsley vinaigrette. For dessert, fruit sorbet topped with a drizzle of chocolate syrup and a few slivered toasted almonds.

FAT: 6G/18%
CALORIES: 305
SATURATED FAT: 1.2G
CARBOHYDRATE: 50G
PROTEIN: 16G
CHOLESTEROL: 26MG
SODIUM: 947MG

BROCCOLI AND POTATO FRITTATA

SERVES: 4
WORKING TIME: 30 MINUTES
TOTAL TIME: 40 MINUTES

1 pound baking potatoes, peeled and cut into small dice

2 cups reduced-sodium chicken broth, defatted

2 whole cloves garlic, peeled, plus 2 cloves garlic, minced

2 teaspoons olive oil

1 medium red onion, coarsely chopped

1 red bell pepper, diced

3 cups small broccoli florets

2 eggs

5 egg whites

⅓ cup grated Parmesan cheese

¼ teaspoon salt

¼ teaspoon freshly ground black pepper

1. In a large saucepan, combine the potatoes, broth, and whole cloves of garlic. Cover and bring to a boil over high heat. Reduce to a simmer and cook until the potatoes are tender, about 10 minutes. Drain, reserving ¼ cup of the cooking liquid. Pat the potatoes dry with paper towels and set aside. Discard the cooked garlic.

2. Meanwhile, preheat the oven to 375°. In a large nonstick oven-proof skillet, heat the oil until hot but not smoking over medium heat. Add the onion and minced garlic and cook, stirring frequently, until the onion is golden brown, about 7 minutes.

3. Add the bell pepper and potatoes, stirring to coat. Cook until the pepper is crisp-tender, about 4 minutes. Stir in the broccoli and cook until the broccoli is tender, about 4 minutes longer.

4. In a small bowl, whisk together the eggs, egg whites, Parmesan, reserved ¼ cup cooking liquid, the salt, and black pepper. Pour the egg mixture over the broccoli mixture and cook without stirring until the bottom is just set, about 4 minutes. Place the skillet in the oven and bake for 7 minutes, or until the frittata is set. Serve from the pan.

Suggested accompaniments: Rye bread, and sliced plum tomatoes with shredded fresh basil and a mustard vinaigrette. For dessert, assorted melon balls tossed with lime juice.

FAT: 7G/26%
CALORIES: 241
SATURATED FAT: 2.3G
CARBOHYDRATE: 28G
PROTEIN: 18G
CHOLESTEROL: 111MG
SODIUM: 714MG

Sunday brunch or a no-fuss family supper—this baked omelet travels easily from stovetop to tabletop, especially if you use an attractive skillet. Made lower in fat with additional egg whites, our frittata gains flavor with broccoli, sweet red pepper, and tangy grated Parmesan. If you don't own an ovenproof skillet, just wrap the handle of a regular nonstick skillet in foil.

Richly flavored and accented with tarragon and hot pepper sauce, this dish makes a colorful presentation for a special dinner. The tasty surprise is the garlic mashed potatoes hidden in the center of the rolled fish fillets. Even better, the potatoes are kept sensibly light by mixing some of the potato cooking water with low-fat milk.

FISH ROLL-UP SUPPER

SERVES: 4
WORKING TIME: 20 MINUTES
TOTAL TIME: 50 MINUTES

1 pound all-purpose potatoes, peeled and thinly sliced

2 whole cloves garlic, peeled, plus 3 cloves garlic, minced

1¾ cups low-fat (1%) milk

½ teaspoon salt

¼ teaspoon freshly ground black pepper

2 teaspoons olive oil

3 scallions, thinly sliced

10-ounce package frozen chopped spinach, thawed and squeezed dry

2 tablespoons fresh lemon juice

½ teaspoon dried tarragon

¼ teaspoon hot pepper sauce

2 tablespoons flour

4 flounder fillets (5 ounces each), any visible bones removed

3 ounces Cheddar cheese, shredded (about ¾ cup)

1 carrot, diced

1 red bell pepper, diced

⅓ cup frozen corn kernels

1. In a large saucepan of boiling water, cook the potatoes and whole cloves of garlic until tender, about 15 minutes. Drain, reserving ¼ cup of the cooking liquid. Transfer the potatoes and garlic to a large bowl. Add ¼ cup of the milk, ¼ teaspoon of the salt, and the pepper and mash the mixture, adding enough of the reserved ¼ cup cooking liquid to make a thick, smooth purée. Set aside.

2. In a large nonstick skillet, heat the oil until hot but not smoking over medium heat. Add the scallions and minced garlic and cook, stirring frequently, until tender, about 4 minutes. Add the spinach, 1 tablespoon of the lemon juice, ¼ teaspoon of the tarragon, the hot pepper sauce, and remaining ¼ teaspoon salt and cook, stirring frequently, for 2 minutes. Stir in the flour until well blended, then gradually add the remaining 1½ cups milk. Bring to a boil, reduce to a simmer, and cook until slightly thickened, about 4 minutes.

3. Lay the fillets flat, skinned-side up. Sprinkle with the remaining 1 tablespoon lemon juice and remaining ¼ teaspoon tarragon, spread the potato purée over, and roll up (see tip). Place the fish rolls, seam-side down, over the spinach mixture, cover, and simmer until the fish is almost opaque, about 9 minutes. Sprinkle with the cheese, carrot, bell pepper, and corn. Cover again; simmer until the fish is opaque and the vegetables are tender, about 4 minutes longer.

Suggested accompaniment: Strawberry compote for dessert.

FAT: 13G/28%
CALORIES: 415
SATURATED FAT: 5.9G
CARBOHYDRATE: 35G
PROTEIN: 41G
CHOLESTEROL: 95MG
SODIUM: 649MG

TIP

To stuff the flounder fillets, after seasoning them with lemon juice and tarragon, spread the potato purée evenly with a spoon. Starting from a short side, neatly roll up each fillet, and then place the fillets seam-side down on the spinach mixture in the skillet.

CHUNKY CHICKEN AND VEGETABLE HASH

SERVES: 4
WORKING TIME: 30 MINUTES
TOTAL TIME: 45 MINUTES

¾ pound small red potatoes, cut into ½-inch dice

1 tablespoon olive oil

1 green bell pepper, diced

1 yellow bell pepper, diced

1 carrot, quartered lengthwise and cut into thin slices

3 scallions, thinly sliced

½ pound skinless, boneless chicken breasts, cut into ½-inch chunks

½ teaspoon salt

½ teaspoon freshly ground black pepper

¼ teaspoon dried rosemary

¾ cup evaporated skimmed milk

3 tablespoons snipped fresh dill

1. In a large saucepan of boiling water, cook the potatoes until just tender, about 10 minutes. Drain well.

2. In a large skillet, heat the oil until hot but not smoking over medium heat. Add the bell peppers, carrot, scallions, and potatoes, stirring to coat. Cook, stirring occasionally, until the peppers and carrot are crisp-tender, about 5 minutes.

3. Stir in the chicken, salt, black pepper, and rosemary and cook, stirring frequently, until the chicken is no longer pink, about 5 minutes.

4. Gradually add the evaporated milk and cook, turning the mixture occasionally, until the hash is nicely crusted and golden brown, about 10 minutes longer. Sprinkle with the dill and serve the hash from the pan.

Suggested accompaniments: Bagel crisps, and hearts of romaine lettuce with a nonfat creamy cucumber dressing.

FAT: 4G/16%
CALORIES: 222
SATURATED FAT: .7G
CARBOHYDRATE: 26G
PROTEIN: 19G
CHOLESTEROL: 35MG
SODIUM: 382MG

Our all-American special is nutritionally updated with evaporated skimmed milk so that it retains the creaminess of the old-style version, but with fewer calories and much less fat. We use the classic poultry seasonings of rosemary and dill, and toss in chopped vegetables for flavor and color. Keep this recipe in mind when you want a filling and attractive brunch dish, too.

Yellow squash and zucchini keep this pasta dish light, as do the meatballs made with ground turkey, lean beef, and a splash of low-fat milk for moistness. When shopping, choose squash that are on the small side because they will be sweeter. You may replace the turkey with ground chicken, and the beef with pork.

Skillet Spaghetti and Meatballs

SERVES: 4
WORKING TIME: 20 MINUTES
TOTAL TIME: 40 MINUTES

¼ pound lean ground beef

¼ pound ground turkey

¼ cup grated Parmesan cheese

2 tablespoons fine plain dried bread crumbs

2 tablespoons low-fat (1%) milk

1 egg white

½ teaspoon dried thyme

½ teaspoon dried sage

¼ teaspoon salt

2 tablespoons flour

2 teaspoons olive oil

14½-ounce can no-salt-added stewed tomatoes, chopped with their juices

2 strips orange zest, each about 3 inches long (see tip)

¾ cup orange juice, preferably fresh

6 ounces thin spaghetti, broken into thirds

1 cup thinly sliced zucchini

1 cup thinly sliced yellow summer squash

1. In a medium bowl, combine the beef, turkey, Parmesan, bread crumbs, milk, egg white, ¼ teaspoon of the thyme, ¼ teaspoon of the sage, and the salt. Mix until well combined and form into 16 meatballs.

2. On a sheet of waxed paper, spread the flour. Dredge the meatballs in the flour, shaking off the excess. In a large nonstick skillet, heat the oil until hot but not smoking over medium heat. Add the meatballs, in batches if necessary, and cook until lightly browned, about 3 minutes.

3. Stir in the tomatoes with their juices, 1¼ cups of water, the orange zest, orange juice, remaining ¼ teaspoon thyme, and remaining ¼ teaspoon sage until well combined. Bring to a boil, reduce to a simmer, cover, and cook until the meatballs are almost cooked through, about 5 minutes.

4. Increase the heat to medium, return to a boil, and stir in the spaghetti, zucchini, and yellow squash. Cover again and cook, stirring occasionally, until the spaghetti is tender and the meatballs are cooked through, about 15 minutes longer. Divide the spaghetti and meatballs among 4 bowls and serve.

Suggested accompaniments: Garlic toasts and, for dessert, a fresh fruit salad garnished with sweetened whipped evaporated skimmed milk.

FAT: 13G/28%
CALORIES: 411
SATURATED FAT: 4.4G
CARBOHYDRATE: 52G
PROTEIN: 21G
CHOLESTEROL: 46MG
SODIUM: 344MG

TIP

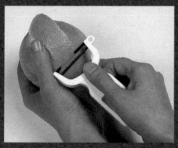

To remove a strip of zest from the orange, use a swivel-bladed vegetable peeler to cut off a piece of the outer colored rind, avoiding the bitter white pith attached to the underside. The zest contains the intensely flavored oil found in the skin.

Spicy Rice with Chicken and Vegetables

Serves: 4
Working time: 25 minutes
Total time: 45 minutes

2 teaspoons olive oil

¼ cup thinly sliced scallions (white and tender green parts only)

3 cloves garlic, minced

1 zucchini, quartered lengthwise and cut into ½-inch-thick slices

1 red bell pepper, diced

1¼ cups medium-hot prepared low-sodium salsa

1 tablespoon fresh lime juice

1 cup long-grain rice

2 cups reduced-sodium chicken broth, defatted

½ teaspoon dried oregano

¼ teaspoon dried thyme

⅛ teaspoon cayenne pepper

½ pound skinless, boneless chicken thighs, cut into 1-inch chunks

2 tablespoons chopped fresh parsley

1. In a large skillet, heat the oil until hot but not smoking over medium heat. Add the scallions and garlic and cook, stirring frequently, until the mixture is softened, about 2 minutes. Add the zucchini and bell pepper and cook, stirring frequently, until the pepper is tender, about 5 minutes. Transfer the vegetable mixture to a medium bowl, stir in the salsa and lime juice, and set aside.

2. Add the rice to the pan, stirring to coat. Stir in the broth, oregano, thyme, and cayenne. Bring to a boil, reduce to a simmer, cover, and cook until the rice is almost tender and the liquid is absorbed, about 12 minutes.

3. Stir in the chicken. Return the vegetable mixture to the pan, stir well, and return to a boil over medium-high heat. Reduce to a simmer, cover again, and cook until the chicken is cooked through and the rice is tender, about 9 minutes longer. Stir in the parsley and serve.

Suggested accompaniments: Iced coffee flavored with cinnamon. For dessert, tapioca pudding made with low-fat milk and studded with brandy-plumped raisins.

A prepared salsa robustly flavors this easy chicken and rice, and oregano and thyme add a subtle fragrance. For a nuttier taste, substitute basmati or Texmati rice for the long-grain white, and for a more pungent finish, chopped cilantro instead of parsley. If reheating leftovers, add a little chicken broth or water beforehand to keep the rice moist.

Fat: 5g/15%
Calories: 297
Saturated Fat: 1g
Carbohydrate: 45g
Protein: 17g
Cholesterol: 47mg
Sodium: 381mg

Meatball are sublimely flavored with dill and yogurt—classic Middle Eastern partners—and combined with pasta and vegetables to create this satisfying supper. Any short, sturdy pasta, such as ziti or penne, will do well here if spinach fusilli is not available. If you don't see lean ground lamb in your meat case, ask the butcher to trim and grind you some, or use lean ground beef.

LAMB MEATBALLS WITH SPINACH FUSILLI

SERVES: 4
WORKING TIME: 20 MINUTES
TOTAL TIME: 40 MINUTES

6 ounces spinach fusilli pasta

½ pound lean ground lamb or beef

⅓ cup minced scallions

¼ cup snipped fresh dill (see tip)

3 tablespoons plain low-fat yogurt

2 tablespoons plain dried bread crumbs

½ teaspoon salt

¼ teaspoon freshly ground black pepper

2 teaspoons olive oil

3 cups cauliflower florets

1 red bell pepper, diced

14½-ounce can no-salt-added stewed tomatoes, chopped with their juices

⅓ cup reduced-sodium chicken broth, defatted

2 tablespoons no-salt-added tomato paste

1. In a large pot of boiling water, cook the fusilli until just tender. Drain well and set aside.

2. Meanwhile, in a medium bowl, combine the lamb, scallions, 2 tablespoons of the dill, the yogurt, bread crumbs, ¼ teaspoon of the salt, and the black pepper. Mix until well combined and form into 12 meatballs. Set aside.

3. In a large skillet, heat the oil until hot but not smoking over medium heat. Add the cauliflower and bell pepper and cook until the cauliflower is lightly golden, about 2 minutes. Stir in the tomatoes with their juices, the broth, tomato paste, remaining 2 tablespoons dill, and remaining ¼ teaspoon salt and bring to a boil. Add the meatballs, reduce to a simmer, cover, and cook until the meatballs are just cooked through, about 9 minutes.

4. Stir in the fusilli and cook, uncovered, until the fusilli is just heated through, about 3 minutes longer. Divide the meatballs, fusilli, and vegetables among 4 bowls and serve.

Suggested accompaniments: Spinach and feta cheese salad with a tarragon vinaigrette, and fresh figs drizzled with honey for dessert.

After rinsing and drying fresh dill, use kitchen shears to snip the feathery fronds directly into a measuring cup, avoiding the stems, until you have the amount the recipe calls for.

FAT: 7G/18%
CALORIES: 343
SATURATED FAT: 2G
CARBOHYDRATE: 49G
PROTEIN: 21G
CHOLESTEROL: 38MG
SODIUM: 456MG

Beef Pilaf

SERVES: 4
WORKING TIME: 25 MINUTES
TOTAL TIME: 50 MINUTES

Many wonderful flavors complement each other in this tantalizing dish—allspice plays nicely against the dried apricots and the basmati rice adds an elusive nuttiness. Chunks of chicken thigh meat or pork loin can be substituted for the beef, or to create a vegetarian side dish, you may omit the meat altogether.

2 tablespoons flour
½ teaspoon salt
¼ teaspoon freshly ground black pepper
¾ pound lean bottom round of beef or lean leg of lamb, cut into ½-inch chunks
2 teaspoons olive oil
1 large onion, diced
4 cloves garlic, minced
2 tablespoons minced fresh ginger
2 carrots, shredded
1 cup basmati or Texmati rice
2 cups reduced-sodium chicken broth, defatted
½ cup dried apricots, slivered
¼ teaspoon red pepper flakes
⅛ teaspoon ground allspice
3 scallions, finely minced
2 tablespoons coarsely chopped almonds, with skins
¼ cup plain nonfat yogurt

1. On a sheet of waxed paper, combine the flour, ¼ teaspoon of the salt, and the black pepper. Dredge the beef in the flour mixture, shaking off the excess. In a large nonstick skillet, heat the oil until hot but not smoking over medium heat. Add the beef and cook, stirring frequently, until browned, about 4 minutes. With a slotted spoon, transfer the beef to a plate and set aside.

2. Add the onion, garlic, and ginger to the pan, stirring to coat. Add ¼ cup of water and cook, stirring frequently, until the onion is softened, about 7 minutes. Add the carrots, stirring to coat. Stir in the rice. Add the broth, apricots, red pepper flakes, allspice, and remaining ¼ teaspoon salt and bring to a boil. Reduce to a simmer, cover, and cook until the rice is almost tender, about 15 minutes.

3. Return the beef to the skillet, cover again, and cook until the beef is just cooked through and the rice is tender, about 4 minutes. Stir in the scallions and almonds and cook, uncovered, until the scallions and almonds are just heated through, about 2 minutes longer. Spoon the beef pilaf onto 4 plates, spoon 1 tablespoon of the yogurt on top of each portion, and serve.

Suggested accompaniments: Watercress and Belgian endive salad with a coriander dressing, and pears poached in vanilla sugar syrup for dessert.

FAT: 10G/21%
CALORIES: 439
SATURATED FAT: 2.2G
CARBOHYDRATE: 62G
PROTEIN: 29G
CHOLESTEROL: 51MG
SODIUM: 696MG

CHICKEN WITH PEANUT SAUCE

SERVES: 4
WORKING TIME: 25 MINUTES
TOTAL TIME: 30 MINUTES

¼ cup chopped fresh basil

3 tablespoons fresh lime juice

2 teaspoons honey

½ pound skinless, boneless chicken breasts, cut into 1-inch pieces

2 teaspoons olive oil

2 red bell peppers, cut into thick strips

½ pound all-purpose potatoes, peeled and cut into ½-inch dice

1¼ cups bottled or canned baby corn

⅔ cup sliced water chestnuts

⅔ cup reduced-sodium chicken broth, defatted

4 cloves garlic, minced

1 tablespoon minced fresh ginger

1 tablespoon reduced-sodium soy sauce

2 teaspoons creamy peanut butter

2 teaspoons cornstarch

¼ cup chopped fresh mint

2 tablespoons chopped fresh cilantro

1. In a medium bowl, combine 2 tablespoons of the basil, 2 tablespoons of the lime juice, and the honey and whisk to blend well. Add the chicken, tossing to coat. Set aside.

2. In a large nonstick skillet, heat the oil until hot but not smoking over medium heat. Add the bell peppers and potatoes and cook, stirring frequently, until the bell peppers are crisp-tender, about 4 minutes. Stir in the corn, water chestnuts, ⅓ cup of the broth, the garlic, and ginger. Bring to a boil, reduce to a simmer, cover, and cook until the potatoes are tender, about 5 minutes.

3. Meanwhile, in a small bowl, whisk together the remaining ⅓ cup broth, the soy sauce, peanut butter, and remaining 1 tablespoon lime juice. Add the chicken with its marinade to the pan and cook uncovered, stirring frequently, until the chicken is no longer pink, about 4 minutes. Stir in the peanut butter mixture and cook until the chicken is cooked through, about 2 minutes.

4. In a cup, combine the cornstarch and 1 tablespoon of water and stir to blend. Bring the chicken mixture to a boil over medium-high heat, stir in the cornstarch mixture along with the mint, cilantro, and remaining 2 tablespoons basil, and cook, stirring constantly, until the mixture is slightly thickened, about 1 minute longer.

Suggested accompaniment: Broiled pineapple rings with grenadine.

FAT: 5G/22%
CALORIES: 208
SATURATED FAT: .7G
CARBOHYDRATE: 25G
PROTEIN: 17G
CHOLESTEROL: 33MG
SODIUM: 322MG

This dish explodes with fresh, sweet, and tangy flavors—honey, basil, mint, lime juice, and cilantro—and it's all tempered with a touch of peanut butter in the sauce. Baby corn and water chestnuts provide an intriguing textural contrast. Because this dish cooks very quickly, be sure to have all the ingredients prepared and ready to go before you begin.

PORK AND BUTTERNUT SQUASH SAUTÉ

SERVES: 4
WORKING TIME: 25 MINUTES
TOTAL TIME: 40 MINUTES

¾ pound small red potatoes, cut into ½-inch dice

2 tablespoons flour

½ teaspoon salt

¼ teaspoon freshly ground black pepper

½ pound lean boneless pork loin, cut into 2-by-¼-inch strips

2 teaspoons olive oil

3 cups peeled, seeded, and cut butternut squash (½-inch chunks)

3 turnips, cut into ½-inch-thick wedges

3 carrots, cut into ½-inch-thick slices

⅔ cup reduced-sodium chicken broth, defatted

¼ cup cider vinegar

½ teaspoon rubbed sage

½ teaspoon ground ginger

2 tablespoons chopped fresh parsley

1. In a large saucepan of boiling water, cook the potatoes until almost tender, about 5 minutes. Drain well and set aside.

2. Meanwhile, on a sheet of waxed paper, combine the flour, ¼ teaspoon of the salt, and ⅛ teaspoon of the pepper. Dredge the pork in the flour mixture, shaking off the excess. In a large skillet, heat the oil until hot but not smoking over medium heat. Add the pork and cook, stirring frequently, until lightly browned, about 3 minutes. With a slotted spoon, transfer the pork to a plate. Set aside.

3. Add the potatoes, squash, turnips, and carrots to the skillet, stirring to coat. Stir in the broth, vinegar, sage, ginger, remaining ¼ teaspoon salt, and remaining ⅛ teaspoon pepper. Bring to a boil, reduce to a simmer, cover, and cook until the vegetables are tender, about 10 minutes.

4. Return the pork to the pan and cook, uncovered, just until the pork is cooked through, about 3 minutes longer. Stir in the parsley and serve.

Suggested accompaniments: Crusty rolls, followed by fresh blueberries swirled into lemon nonfat yogurt.

FAT: 6G/19%
CALORIES: 284
SATURATED FAT: 1.4G
CARBOHYDRATE: 43G
PROTEIN: 17G
CHOLESTEROL: 33MG
SODIUM: 499MG

Sage and ground ginger are the perfect seasonings to highlight the sweetness of the butternut squash and root vegetables in this hearty fall dish, and the cider vinegar accents the richness of the pork. As a bonus, this dish tastes just as good—if not better—if prepared a day ahead. Reheat, covered, on the stovetop over low heat or in the microwave.

MILANESE-STYLE RICE

SERVES: 4
WORKING TIME: 40 MINUTES
TOTAL TIME: 1 HOUR

*P*eas
and mushrooms create
the Milanese style in
this creamy rice dish,
a delicious and
simplified variation of
the classic risotto.

2 teaspoons olive oil

½ pound skinless, boneless chicken thighs, cut into ½-inch pieces

1 large onion, coarsely chopped

½ pound mushrooms, thickly sliced

2 cups reduced-sodium chicken broth, defatted

1½ cups long-grain rice

⅔ cup dry white wine

¼ teaspoon freshly ground black pepper

1½ cups frozen peas, thawed

⅔ cup grated Parmesan cheese

¼ cup chopped fresh parsley

1. In a large nonstick skillet, heat the oil until hot but not smoking over medium heat. Add the chicken and cook, stirring frequently, until golden brown, about 5 minutes. With a slotted spoon, transfer the chicken to a plate and set aside.

2. Add the onion to the pan and cook, stirring frequently, until the onion is golden brown and very tender, about 10 minutes. Add the mushrooms and ¼ cup of the broth and cook, stirring frequently, until the mushrooms are lightly browned, about 5 minutes.

3. Add the rice, stirring to coat. Stir in the wine and cook, stirring occasionally, until the liquid has evaporated, about 7 minutes. Stir in the remaining 1¾ cups broth, 1 cup of water, and the black pepper. Bring to a boil, reduce to a simmer, cover, and cook until the rice is tender, about 17 minutes.

4. Return the chicken to the pan, cover again, and cook until the chicken is just cooked through, about 2 minutes. Stir in the peas, Parmesan, and parsley and cook, uncovered, until the rice is creamy and the peas are heated through, about 3 minutes longer. Spoon the rice mixture onto 4 plates and serve.

Suggested accompaniments: Roasted red pepper salad with a lemon dressing, and chocolate ice milk with chocolate shavings afterward.

FAT: 9G/16%
CALORIES: 491
SATURATED FAT: 3.6G
CARBOHYDRATE: 72G
PROTEIN: 28G
CHOLESTEROL: 58MG
SODIUM: 692MG

OVEN DINNERS

3

To brighten the flavor of plain roast chicken, we've rubbed a mixture of lemon juice, garlic, and rosemary beneath the skin. The herb mixture stays on the chicken itself instead of being lost on the skin, which gets removed before eating. To reduce fat even more, we've placed the chicken on a rack set over a roasting pan so the fat drips away into the pan.

Roast Chicken Dinner

Serves: 4
Working time: 20 minutes
Total time: 1 hour 35 minutes

¼ cup fresh lemon juice

3 cloves garlic, minced

2 tablespoons dried rosemary

2 teaspoons olive oil

¾ teaspoon salt

¼ teaspoon freshly ground black pepper

3-pound chicken

1 pound small red potatoes, halved

3 carrots, halved lengthwise

2 medium onions, halved lengthwise

2 yellow summer squash, halved lengthwise

1. Preheat the oven to 425°. In a small bowl, combine the lemon juice, garlic, rosemary, oil, salt, and pepper. With your fingers, carefully loosen the skin from the chicken breast, leaving the skin intact. Spread half of the lemon-herb mixture under the skin (see tip). Truss the chicken by tying the legs together with string.

2. In a large bowl, combine the potatoes, carrots, onions, and squash, drizzle with the remaining lemon-herb mixture, and toss to coat. Place the chicken, breast-side down, on a rack in a large roasting pan, arrange the potatoes and carrots around the chicken, and roast for 30 minutes.

3. Turn the potatoes and carrots. Add the onions and squash to the pan and continue to roast, basting the chicken occasionally with the pan juices, for 20 minutes.

4. Turn all the vegetables. Turn the chicken breast-side up, and continue to roast, basting occasionally, for 30 minutes longer, or until the chicken is cooked through and the vegetables are tender. Transfer the chicken and vegetables to a serving platter. Remove the skin from the chicken before eating.

Suggested accompaniment: For dessert, rice pudding made with low-fat milk and dusted with cinnamon.

Fat: 15g/29%
Calories: 448
Saturated Fat: 3.6g
Carbohydrate: 40g
Protein: 40g
Cholesterol: 120mg
Sodium: 571mg

TIP

To place seasonings under the skin of a chicken, loosen the edges of the skin along the breasts at the back end of the bird. Gently separate the skin from the meat on both sides of the breast, forming a pocket. Push the seasoning mixture into the pocket, spreading it evenly over the meat. Then ease the skin back to cover the mixture.

BAKED RIGATONI WITH VEGETABLES

SERVES: 4
WORKING TIME: 25 MINUTES
TOTAL TIME: 55 MINUTES

12 ounces rigatoni pasta

2 teaspoons olive oil

1 large onion, diced

2 cloves garlic, minced

1 red bell pepper, diced

1 cup broccoli florets

1 cup frozen corn kernels

1½ cups no-salt-added tomato sauce

1 cup part-skim ricotta cheese

½ cup low-fat (1%) cottage cheese

2 tablespoons grated Parmesan cheese

½ teaspoon salt

¼ teaspoon freshly ground black pepper

2 tablespoons chopped fresh parsley

1. Preheat the oven to 350°. In a large pot of boiling water, cook the rigatoni until just tender. Drain well and set aside.

2. Meanwhile, in a large nonstick skillet, heat the oil until hot but not smoking over medium heat. Add the onion and garlic and cook, stirring frequently, until the onion is slightly softened, about 5 minutes. Add the bell pepper, broccoli, and corn and cook until the pepper and broccoli are crisp-tender, about 3 minutes longer. Remove from the heat.

3. In a large bowl, stir together the tomato sauce, ricotta, cottage cheese, and Parmesan. Stir in the vegetable mixture, salt, and black pepper. Add the rigatoni and toss well to combine.

4. Spoon the rigatoni mixture into a 12 x 8-inch baking dish. Cover with foil and bake for 30 minutes, or until the casserole is piping hot. Sprinkle with the parsley and serve.

Suggested accompaniments: Escarole and sliced cucumber salad with a nonfat Italian dressing. Follow with fresh pineapple wedges.

Who can resist this delicious pasta casserole? The sauce is creamy, but we've trimmed the fat by using part-skim ricotta cheese and low-fat cottage cheese.

When you buy broccoli, make sure the florets are tight and green, with no yellow patches. Experiment with other vegetables here as well, including zucchini, cauliflower, peas, yellow squash, and lima beans.

FAT: 10G/17%
CALORIES: 558
SATURATED FAT: 4.2G
CARBOHYDRATE: 91G
PROTEIN: 27G
CHOLESTEROL: 22MG
SODIUM: 548MG

OPEN-FACE EGGPLANT AND PESTO SANDWICHES

SERVES: 4
WORKING TIME: 25 MINUTES
TOTAL TIME: 55 MINUTES

Looking sinfully rich, these sandwiches actually fit into a sensible eating plan, thanks to a few low-fat tricks. The eggplant slices are not fried but baked, bathed in a piquant blend of broth and balsamic vinegar. And the smooth sauce is a mix of low-fat cottage cheese and Parmesan, lightened with egg whites and aggressively seasoned with garlic and fresh basil.

1 tablespoon olive oil

1 teaspoon dried oregano

⅛ teaspoon cayenne pepper

8 slices (½ ounce each) whole-wheat Italian bread

1 clove garlic, halved, plus 1 clove garlic, minced

½ cup reduced-sodium chicken broth, defatted

1 tablespoon balsamic or red wine vinegar

1 eggplant (about 1 pound), peeled and cut crosswise into ⅜-inch-thick slices

1 cup low-fat (1%) cottage cheese

2 tablespoons grated Parmesan cheese

½ cup packed fresh basil leaves

2 egg whites

2 tomatoes, thickly sliced

1. Preheat the oven to 400°. In a cup, stir together the oil, oregano, and cayenne. Rub the bread with the cut sides of the halved garlic clove, then brush with the oil mixture. Place the bread on a baking sheet and set aside.

2. Spray another baking sheet with nonstick cooking spray. In a small bowl, combine the broth and vinegar. Arrange the eggplant slices on the prepared baking sheet and brush with half of the broth mixture. Place the bread and eggplant in the oven and bake for 10 minutes, or until the bread is crisp, turning the bread after 5 minutes. Set the bread aside. Brush the eggplant with the remaining broth mixture and bake for 5 minutes longer, or until the eggplant is tender.

3. Meanwhile, in a food processor or blender, purée the cottage cheese, Parmesan, minced garlic, basil, and egg whites until smooth. Arrange the bread in a single layer in a 13 x 9-inch baking pan and place the tomatoes on top. Place the eggplant over the tomatoes, spoon the cottage cheese purée on top, and bake for 20 minutes, or until the sandwiches are piping hot. Place the sandwiches on 4 plates and serve.

Suggested accompaniment: For dessert, mixed berries topped with a dollop of mango nonfat yogurt and a few chopped toasted macadamia nuts.

FAT: 7G/28%
CALORIES: 213
SATURATED FAT: 1.6G
CARBOHYDRATE: 27G
PROTEIN: 15G
CHOLESTEROL: 4MG
SODIUM: 544MG

A surprisingly simple dish to prepare, this is special enough for a pull-out-all-the-stops dinner party. We pair the salmon with its natural flavor partners, dill and lemon, and then display the fish on a bed of colorful vegetables. Baking the salmon with the skin on allows it to hold its shape (for presentation, we remove the skin just before serving).

Baked Salmon on a Bed of Vegetables

Serves: 4
Working time: 30 minutes
Total time: 1 hour 10 minutes

¼ cup plus 1 tablespoon snipped fresh dill

2 tablespoons fresh lemon juice

¼ teaspoon salt

¼ teaspoon freshly ground black pepper

2 salmon fillets with skin (about 10 ounces each), any visible bones removed

4 carrots, cut into 2-inch julienne strips

3 leeks (white and light green parts only), cut into 2-inch julienne strips

1 pound baking potatoes, peeled and cut into 2-inch julienne strips

2 teaspoons olive oil

1. Preheat the oven to 400°. In a small bowl, combine ¼ cup of the dill, the lemon juice, ⅛ teaspoon of the salt, and ⅛ teaspoon of the pepper. Lay the salmon fillets flat, skin-side down. Spoon half of the dill mixture on top of each fillet. Carefully press the dill-covered sides of the salmon together. Set aside.

2. In a large bowl, combine the carrots, leeks, and potatoes. Add the oil, remaining 1 tablespoon dill, remaining ⅛ teaspoon salt, and remaining ⅛ teaspoon pepper and toss well to combine. Spread the vegetables in a 14 x 10-inch roasting pan. Place the salmon on top, keeping the dill-covered sides together, cover with foil, and bake for 20 minutes.

3. Remove the foil and gently stir the vegetables. Replace the foil and continue to bake for 20 minutes longer, or until the salmon is just opaque and the vegetables are tender.

4. Transfer the salmon to a cutting board and separate the fillets. Remove and discard the skin (see tip; top photo), turn the salmon dill-covered side up, then cut each fillet crosswise in half (bottom photo). Divide the vegetable mixture among 4 plates and place the salmon on top, dill-covered side up. Drizzle any pan juices over the salmon and serve.

Suggested accompaniment: End with reduced-fat cherry cheesecake.

Fat: 12g/28%
Calories: 376
Saturated Fat: 1.8g
Carbohydrate: 36g
Protein: 32g
Cholesterol: 78mg
Sodium: 247mg

TIP

Using a small, sharp paring knife, carefully trim off the salmon skin, keeping the blade as close to the skin as possible. Turn the salmon, dill-covered side up, and cut each fillet crosswise in half to make four generous servings.

PORK WITH POTATOES AND ARTICHOKES

SERVES: 4
WORKING TIME: 20 MINUTES
TOTAL TIME: 1 HOUR

dry rub of garlic, bay leaf, and sage infuses the lean, tender pork with robust flavor, without the fat of an oil-based marinade.

1½ pounds small new potatoes, cut into ½-inch chunks

9-ounce package frozen artichoke hearts

3 carrots, cut into 2-inch julienne

1 cup reduced-sodium chicken broth, defatted

¼ cup fresh lemon juice

2 teaspoons olive oil

2 cloves garlic, minced

1 bay leaf, crushed

½ teaspoon rubbed sage

¼ teaspoon salt

10 ounces lean boneless pork loin

¼ cup chopped fresh parsley

1. Preheat the oven to 400°. In a large pot of boiling water, cook the potatoes for 6 minutes. Add the artichokes and carrots and cook for 2 minutes longer (the vegetables will not be completely tender). Drain well and transfer the vegetables to a large bowl. Add the broth, lemon juice, and oil and toss well to coat. Spread the vegetables in a small baking pan and bake for 10 minutes.

2. Meanwhile, in a small bowl, combine the garlic, bay leaf, sage, and salt. Rub the pork all over with the garlic-herb mixture. Place the pork on top of the vegetables, cover with foil, and bake for 15 minutes.

3. Remove the foil and continue to bake for 10 minutes longer, or until the pork is cooked through and the vegetables are tender.

4. Transfer the pork to a cutting board and let stand for 5 minutes. Sprinkle the parsley over the vegetables and toss to combine. Cut the pork into thin slices. Divide the pork and vegetables among 4 plates and serve.

Suggested accompaniment: Poached Bartlett pear halves sprinkled with crumbled macaroons.

FAT: 7G/20%
CALORIES: 319
SATURATED FAT: 1.7G
CARBOHYDRATE: 44G
PROTEIN: 22G
CHOLESTEROL: 42MG
SODIUM: 397MG

Meat Loaf Blue Plate Special

SERVES: 4
WORKING TIME: 35 MINUTES
TOTAL TIME: 1 HOUR 5 MINUTES

2 slices white bread, crumbled

¼ cup skim milk

¾ pound extra-lean ground beef

2 cups grated carrots

1 rib celery, finely chopped

1 medium onion, minced

2 cloves garlic, minced, plus 4 cloves garlic, sliced

½ cup no-salt-added stewed tomatoes, drained and chopped

1 egg white, slightly beaten

1 teaspoon dried thyme

1 teaspoon salt

¼ teaspoon ground black pepper

2 pounds baking potatoes, peeled and thinly sliced

2 teaspoons olive oil

2 tablespoons flour

1 cup reduced-sodium chicken broth, defatted

1 teaspoon Worcestershire sauce

1. Preheat the oven to 400°. Line a small roasting pan with foil. In a large bowl, combine the bread and milk. Add the beef, 1 cup of the carrots, the celery, onion, minced garlic, tomatoes, egg white, ½ teaspoon of the thyme, ½ teaspoon of the salt, and the pepper. Mix well. Transfer to the prepared pan, shape into an 8½-by-4½-inch loaf, and bake for 25 minutes, or until cooked through.

2. Meanwhile, in a large saucepan, combine the potatoes, remaining 1 cup carrots, the sliced garlic, and remaining ½ teaspoon thyme. Add water to cover by 1 inch. Bring to a boil, reduce to a simmer, and cook until the potatoes and carrots are tender, about 20 minutes. Drain, reserving 1¼ cups of the cooking liquid. Transfer the potato mixture to a large bowl. Add ¼ cup of the reserved cooking liquid, the oil, and remaining ½ teaspoon salt and mash the mixture until smooth.

3. With 2 spatulas, transfer the meat loaf to a serving platter. Remove the foil, letting the meat juices drip into the roasting pan. Set the roasting pan over medium heat, add the flour, and cook, stirring constantly, until golden, about 1 minute. Gradually add the broth and remaining 1 cup cooking liquid and cook until the gravy is thickened, about 4 minutes. Stir in the Worcestershire sauce. Thinly slice the meat loaf and serve with the potatoes and gravy.

Suggested accompaniment: Steamed green beans sprinkled with parsley.

FAT: 12G/25%
CALORIES: 420
SATURATED FAT: 3.9G
CARBOHYDRATE: 55G
PROTEIN: 27G
CHOLESTEROL: 53MG
SODIUM: 921MG

*W*e've made this American favorite even better with lots of delicious vegetables and a hearty low-fat gravy.

CREAMY PENNE, BACON, AND VEGETABLE BAKE

SERVES: 4
WORKING TIME: 15 MINUTES
TOTAL TIME: 40 MINUTES

3 cups broccoli florets

2 red bell peppers, diced

8 ounces penne pasta

1½ cups low-fat (1%) cottage cheese

1 cup evaporated skimmed milk

⅔ cup part-skim ricotta cheese

¼ cup plus 2 tablespoons grated Parmesan cheese

2 tablespoons flour

1 egg

¼ cup chopped fresh parsley

½ teaspoon freshly ground black pepper

2 ounces Canadian bacon, diced

1. Preheat the oven to 375°. In a large pot of boiling water, cook the broccoli and bell peppers until crisp-tender, about 2 minutes. Reserve the boiling water for the penne and, with a slotted spoon, transfer the vegetables to a colander to drain. Rinse under cold water and drain again. Cook the penne in the reserved boiling water until just tender. Drain well. Return the penne, broccoli, and bell peppers to the cooking pot and set aside.

2. In a blender or food processor, purée the cottage cheese, evaporated milk, ricotta, ¼ cup of the Parmesan, the flour, and egg until smooth, about 1 minute. Add the parsley and black pepper and purée until well combined. Pour the purée over the penne mixture, add the bacon, and toss well to combine.

3. Spray a 2-quart baking dish with nonstick cooking spray. Spoon the penne mixture into the prepared baking dish, cover with foil, and bake for 15 to 20 minutes, or until the casserole is bubbly and piping hot. Remove the foil, sprinkle the remaining 2 tablespoons Parmesan over, and bake for 4 minutes longer, or until the cheese is lightly golden.

Suggested accompaniments: Tossed green salad with a basil vinaigrette, and assorted reduced-fat cookies with hazelnut coffee for dessert.

FAT: 10G/18%
CALORIES: 511
SATURATED FAT: 4.9G
CARBOHYDRATE: 66G
PROTEIN: 39G
CHOLESTEROL: 85MG
SODIUM: 854MG

This flavorful baked version of spaghetti carbonara captures all the richness of the original, but with much less fat. Low-fat cheeses and lean Canadian bacon are the secrets. You can assemble the casserole several hours ahead and refrigerate it, allowing a little extra baking time for the chilled dish. Buy Parmesan in chunks and store in the freezer, then freshly grate as needed.

HEARTY CASSOULET

SERVES: 4
WORKING TIME: 25 MINUTES
TOTAL TIME: 1 HOUR

4 cloves garlic, minced

½ cup chopped fresh parsley

¼ cup thinly sliced scallions

½ teaspoon dried thyme

¼ teaspoon salt

¼ teaspoon freshly ground black pepper

4 bone-in chicken thighs (about 4 ounces each), skinned

1 teaspoon olive oil

3 carrots, thinly sliced

Two 16-ounce cans white kidney beans (cannellini), rinsed and drained

⅓ cup no-salt-added tomato paste

2 ounces Canadian bacon, diced

1. In a large bowl, stir together the garlic, ¼ cup of the parsley, the scallions, thyme, salt, and pepper. Add the chicken and toss well to coat. Let the mixture stand for 10 minutes before starting the dish.

2. Preheat the oven to 400°. In a large skillet, heat the oil until hot but not smoking over medium heat. Add the carrots and cook, stirring frequently, until the carrots are tender, about 5 minutes.

3. Transfer the carrots to a 1½-quart baking dish. Stir in the chicken mixture, beans, tomato paste, and bacon. Add 1 cup of water and stir until well combined. Cover with foil and bake for 35 minutes, or until the chicken is cooked through and the beans are piping hot. Sprinkle the remaining ¼ cup parsley on top and serve.

Suggested accompaniments: Peasant bread, and watercress and romaine salad with a mustard vinaigrette.

FAT: 6G/17%
CALORIES: 320
SATURATED FAT: 1.2G
CARBOHYDRATE: 37G
PROTEIN: 29G
CHOLESTEROL: 61MG
SODIUM: 710MG

Here is our streamlined interpretation of the long-baking French farmhouse classic. The usual fat-laden meats are replaced with much leaner chicken thighs. And for ease of preparation, we've used canned beans to eliminate the overnight soaking. Just a small amount of Canadian bacon adds big flavor, nicely complemented by the aromatic thyme and scallions.

We

pep up the filling for
these nicely spiced
enchiladas with our
version of a Mexican
mole sauce, using cocoa
powder and flour to
thicken low-fat milk.
If you wish to increase
the "flames" in this
dish, use a hot variety
of canned chilies and a
hot salsa. You may
prefer not to use the
cilantro—the recipe
is still delicious
without it.

CHICKEN ENCHILADAS

SERVES: 4
WORKING TIME: 25 MINUTES
TOTAL TIME: 55 MINUTES

Six 8-inch flour tortillas

1 cup low-fat (1%) milk

2 tablespoons flour

1½ teaspoons ground coriander

1 teaspoon unsweetened cocoa powder

4 scallions, sliced (white and green parts kept separate)

1 pound skinless, boneless chicken breasts, cut into thin strips

4 teaspoons chili powder

2 teaspoons olive oil

1 cup frozen corn kernels

4-ounce can chopped mild green chilies, drained

½ cup chopped fresh cilantro

½ cup medium-hot prepared salsa

½ cup no-salt-added tomato sauce

2 ounces Monterey jack or Cheddar cheese, shredded (about ½ cup)

1. Preheat the oven to 375°. Wrap the tortillas in foil and heat in the oven for 10 minutes, or until warmed through.

2. Meanwhile, in a jar with a tight-fitting lid, shake together the milk, flour, coriander, cocoa, and scallion whites until smooth. Set aside. In a medium bowl, combine the chicken and chili powder and toss to coat. In a large nonstick skillet, heat the oil until hot but not smoking over medium-high heat. Add the chicken and cook, stirring frequently, until the chicken is lightly browned, about 4 minutes.

3. Stir in the milk mixture and bring to a boil. Cook, stirring constantly, until the mixture is slightly thickened, about 3 minutes. Add the scallion greens, corn, and chilies and cook, stirring, until the flavors have blended, about 2 minutes longer. Remove from the heat and stir in ¼ cup of the cilantro.

4. Spray an 11 x 7-inch baking dish with nonstick cooking spray. Unwrap the tortillas and spoon one-sixth of the chicken mixture down the center of each (see tip; top photo). Roll up the tortillas (bottom photo) and place, seam-side down, in the prepared baking dish. In a small bowl, stir together the salsa, tomato sauce, and remaining ¼ cup cilantro and spoon over the tortillas. Sprinkle the cheese on top and bake for 25 minutes, or until piping hot.

Suggested accompaniment: Chocolate nonfat frozen yogurt for dessert.

FAT: 14G/25%
CALORIES: 487
SATURATED FAT: 4.2G
CARBOHYDRATE: 52G
PROTEIN: 39G
CHOLESTEROL: 83MG
SODIUM: 960MG

TIP

Spoon some of the filling evenly down the center of each tortilla, leaving a border on each end to prevent any from spilling out. Roll up the tortilla around the filling, keeping the tortilla tight so the filling remains in a compact cylinder.

PAPER-WRAPPED CHICKEN AND VEGETABLES

SERVES: 4
WORKING TIME: 20 MINUTES
TOTAL TIME: 50 MINUTES

¾ pound small red potatoes, thinly sliced

¼ cup chopped fresh parsley

2 tablespoons coarse-grained mustard

2 teaspoons olive oil

¼ cup orange juice

1 teaspoon grated orange zest

1 teaspoon finely chopped fresh tarragon or 1 tablespoon finely chopped fresh basil

⅛ teaspoon freshly ground black pepper

3 cups sliced mushrooms

1 cup julienned carrots

2 scallions, thinly sliced on the diagonal

4 small skinless, boneless chicken breast halves (about 4 ounces each)

3 ounces Canadian bacon, thinly slivered

1½ tablespoons tarragon sprigs or 4 small basil leaves

1. Preheat the oven to 400°. Cut four 10-inch sheets of parchment paper or foil. In a large saucepan of boiling water, cook the potatoes until almost tender, about 10 minutes. Drain well and transfer to a medium bowl. Add the parsley, mustard, and oil and toss to coat. Add the orange juice, orange zest, chopped tarragon, and pepper and toss to combine.

2. Arrange one-quarter of the potatoes in the center of each parchment sheet. Top with the mushrooms, carrots, and scallions, dividing evenly. Place the chicken on top, sprinkle with the bacon, and top with the tarragon sprigs, dividing evenly. Fold the parchment over the filling and crimp the edges to seal. Place the packets on a baking sheet and bake for 25 to 30 minutes, or until the chicken is cooked through.

3. Place the packets on 4 plates. Cut a cross in the center of each packet, carefully pull back the paper (the mixture may steam), and serve.

Suggested accompaniments: Crusty baguette and cherry tomatoes. For dessert, sliced peaches sautéed with brown sugar.

FAT: 6G/19%
CALORIES: 292
SATURATED FAT: 1.2G
CARBOHYDRATE: 24G
PROTEIN: 34G
CHOLESTEROL: 76MG
SODIUM: 470MG

*A*s the chicken and vegetables steam, sealed in the parchment paper, they cook in their own juices and are perfumed with the flavors of orange and tarragon. Parchment paper makes the best presentation, but foil could easily be substituted. When buying white button mushrooms, select those with unblemished, tight caps.

In our luscious version of the Mediterranean classic, we've used low-fat milk and part-skim mozzarella to keep the sauce deliciously low in fat. Orzo, a rice-shaped pasta, not only replaces the usual ground meat but also adds a creamy texture. Select eggplants that feel heavy for their size, with tight, shiny, blemish-free skins.

Vegetarian Moussaka

SERVES: 4
WORKING TIME: 30 MINUTES
TOTAL TIME: 1 HOUR

½ cup reduced-sodium chicken broth, defatted

2 tablespoons red wine vinegar

2 eggplants (about 8 ounces each), cut lengthwise into ¼-inch-thick slices

8 ounces orzo

2 teaspoons olive oil

1 large onion, coarsely chopped

5 cloves garlic, minced

2 tablespoons flour

1½ cups low-fat (1%) milk

3 ounces part-skim mozzarella cheese, shredded (about ¾ cup)

½ teaspoon dried oregano

½ teaspoon dried rosemary

½ teaspoon salt

¼ teaspoon freshly ground black pepper

8-ounce can no-salt-added tomato sauce

1. Preheat the oven to 425°. Spray 2 baking sheets with nonstick cooking spray. In a large bowl, combine the broth and vinegar. Add the eggplants, tossing to coat. Arrange the eggplant slices on the prepared baking sheets and bake for 15 minutes, or until soft.

2. Meanwhile, in a large pot of boiling water, cook the orzo until just tender. Drain well and set aside.

3. In a large saucepan, heat the oil until hot but not smoking over medium heat. Add the onion and garlic and cook, stirring frequently, until the onion is softened, about 7 minutes. Add the flour and cook, stirring constantly, until lightly golden, about 4 minutes. Gradually whisk in the milk and cook, whisking frequently, until the mixture is slightly thickened, about 4 minutes longer. Remove from the heat and stir in the orzo, all but 2 tablespoons of the mozzarella, the oregano, rosemary, salt, and pepper.

4. Spray a 9 x 9-inch baking dish with nonstick cooking spray. Line 2 sides of the prepared baking dish with the eggplant slices, leaving a 2-inch overhang (see tip). Spoon the orzo mixture over the eggplant, fold the eggplant ends over the mixture, and pour the tomato sauce on top. Bake for 20 minutes, or until the moussaka is piping hot. Sprinkle the remaining 2 tablespoons mozzarella on top and bake for 2 minutes longer, or until the cheese is melted.

Suggested accompaniment: Spinach salad with a citrus vinaigrette.

FAT: 9G/19%
CALORIES: 423
SATURATED FAT: 3.2G
CARBOHYDRATE: 68G
PROTEIN: 19G
CHOLESTEROL: 16MG
SODIUM: 522MG

TIP

Line the baking dish with the eggplant slices so they slightly overlap, leaving a two-inch overhang at the opposite sides of the dish. After the orzo filling has been spooned into the dish, fold the overhang over the top of the filling.

GOLDEN CHICKEN AND CORN CASSEROLE

SERVES: 4
WORKING TIME: 25 MINUTES
TOTAL TIME: 45 MINUTES

2 tablespoons plus ½ cup flour

1 cup reduced-sodium chicken broth, defatted

2 red bell peppers, cut into ½-inch squares

2¾ cups frozen corn kernels, thawed

1 cup minced scallions

2 teaspoons minced pickled jalapeño pepper

½ teaspoon dried rosemary

¾ pound skinless, boneless chicken thighs, cut into 1-inch chunks

½ cup yellow cornmeal

1 teaspoon sugar

1 teaspoon baking powder

½ teaspoon baking soda

¼ teaspoon salt

⅔ cup plain nonfat yogurt

1 egg white

1 tablespoon olive oil

1. Preheat the oven to 400°. Place 2 tablespoons of the flour in a large skillet over medium heat, and gradually whisk in the broth. Bring to a boil and stir in the bell peppers, 1½ cups of the corn, ⅔ cup of the scallions, the jalapeño pepper, and rosemary. Return to a boil, add the chicken, and cook, stirring frequently, for 2 minutes. Spoon the mixture into an 11 x 7-inch baking dish.

2. In a medium bowl, combine the cornmeal, remaining ½ cup flour, the sugar, baking powder, baking soda, and salt. In a small bowl, stir together the yogurt, egg white, and oil. Stir the yogurt mixture into the cornmeal mixture until just combined. Gently fold in the remaining 1¼ cups corn and remaining ⅓ cup scallions.

3. Spoon the cornmeal mixture over the chicken mixture, smoothing the top, and bake for 20 minutes, or until the chicken is cooked through and the crust is golden brown. Divide the casserole among 4 plates and serve.

Suggested accompaniments: Tomato wedges drizzled with tarragon vinegar. For dessert, angel food cake with a little butterscotch sauce.

This deeply satisfying casserole packs a double hit of corn—whole kernels and cornmeal. The topping tastes rich, but nonfat yogurt and an egg white keep the fat content in check. When fresh sweet corn is in season, by all means use it rather than the frozen. Feel free to adjust the amount of pickled jalapeño to suit your taste.

FAT: 8G/18%
CALORIES: 418
SATURATED FAT: 1.5G
CARBOHYDRATE: 61G
PROTEIN: 28G
CHOLESTEROL: 71MG
SODIUM: 721MG

ASPARAGUS STRATA

SERVES: 4
WORKING TIME: 25 MINUTES
TOTAL TIME: 1 HOUR 45 MINUTES (INCLUDES STANDING)

A strata is nothing more than a layered bread casserole. This easy and appealing one is ideal for brunch or supper and, as a bonus, it can be assembled overnight and baked shortly before serving. If you have only very fresh French bread, lightly toast it in the oven to avoid a soggy strata. And if French bread is not available, day-old bakery white bread makes a fine substitute.

6 ounces thin asparagus, tough ends trimmed, cut into ¾-inch pieces

1 red bell pepper, diced

2 cups skim milk

¼ cup grated Parmesan cheese

5 egg whites

1 egg

1 clove garlic, minced

1 tablespoon flour

2 teaspoons dry mustard

1 teaspoon dried oregano

¼ teaspoon freshly ground black pepper

16 slices (½ ounce each) day-old French bread

1 ounce Canadian bacon, thinly slivered

2 ounces Cheddar cheese, shredded (about ½ cup)

1. In a large saucepan of boiling water, cook the asparagus for 4 minutes. Add the bell pepper and cook until the asparagus and pepper are just crisp-tender, about 2 minutes longer. Drain well and set aside.

2. Meanwhile, in a blender or food processor, purée the milk, Parmesan, egg whites, egg, garlic, flour, mustard, oregano, and black pepper until smooth, about 1 minute.

3. Spray a 9 x 9-inch baking dish with nonstick cooking spray. Arrange 8 of the bread slices in a single layer in the prepared baking dish and sprinkle with half of the asparagus mixture. Top with half of the bacon, then sprinkle with half of the Cheddar. Repeat with the remaining bread, asparagus mixture, bacon, and Cheddar. Gradually pour the milk mixture over, cover, and refrigerate for 30 minutes (or, if desired, for up to 1 day).

4. Preheat the oven to 350°. Bake the strata, uncovered, for 45 minutes, or until the top is golden and a knife inserted in the center comes out clean. Divide the strata among 4 plates and serve.

Suggested accompaniment: Fresh fruit salad topped with a scoop of strawberry sherbet.

FAT: 11G/27%
CALORIES: 358
SATURATED FAT: 5G
CARBOHYDRATE: 41G
PROTEIN: 24G
CHOLESTEROL: 78MG
SODIUM: 776MG

TURKEY ORLOFF CASSEROLE

SERVES: 4
WORKING TIME: 20 MINUTES
TOTAL TIME: 50 MINUTES

2 medium onions, finely chopped

10 ounces mushrooms, finely chopped

¾ cup long-grain rice

1 tablespoon julienned lemon zest

½ teaspoon dried tarragon

½ cup low-fat (1.5%) buttermilk

⅓ cup reduced-fat sour cream

½ pound thinly sliced smoked turkey

¼ teaspoon freshly ground black pepper

Two 10-ounce packages frozen chopped broccoli, thawed and squeezed dry

3 tablespoons grated Parmesan cheese

1. In a large saucepan, combine the onions, mushrooms, 1½ cups of water, the rice, lemon zest, and tarragon. Bring to a boil over high heat, reduce to a simmer, cover, and cook for 10 minutes. Remove from the heat and let stand, covered, until the rice is almost tender, about 5 minutes.

2. Meanwhile, preheat the oven to 375°. In a small bowl, stir together the buttermilk and sour cream until smooth. Set aside.

3. Spray a 2½-quart baking dish with nonstick cooking spray. Sprinkle the turkey with the pepper. Place half of the broccoli in the prepared baking dish, lay half of the turkey slices on top, and spoon half of the rice mixture over. Repeat with the remaining broccoli, turkey, and rice mixture. Spoon the buttermilk mixture over, sprinkle the Parmesan on top, and cover with foil. Bake for 25 minutes, or until the casserole is piping hot.

4. Preheat the broiler. Remove the foil and broil the casserole 4 inches from the heat for 3 minutes, or until the top is golden brown.

Suggested accompaniments: Mixed green and red leaf lettuce salad with a reduced-fat poppy seed dressing. Follow with apple slices and currants sautéed with a splash of bourbon.

FAT: 7G/19%
CALORIES: 346
SATURATED FAT: 3.2G
CARBOHYDRATE: 49G
PROTEIN: 24G
CHOLESTEROL: 41MG
SODIUM: 701MG

Here we've lightened the classic French veal Orloff by using lean turkey instead of veal, and buttermilk and reduced-fat sour cream instead of heavy cream in the sauce. For a taste twist, substitute a nutty basmati or Texmati rice for the long-grain white. To get a jump on dinner, assemble the casserole early in the day, refrigerate it, and then just add a few minutes to the baking time.

Wagon Wheels with Spinach-Basil Sauce

Serves: 4
Working time: 30 minutes
Total time: 50 minutes

Whenever luxurious bunches of basil are available— that's the ideal time to prepare this recipe. The wagon wheels add a whimsical touch, but fusilli, rigatoni, or ziti would be equally tasty. We scatter pine nuts over the top for crunch and flavor, but because of their high fat content, we use them sparingly. Store the pine nuts in the freezer for up to six months.

1 red bell pepper, diced

8 ounces ruote (wagon wheel) pasta

2 tablespoons flour

2½ cups low-fat (1%) milk

½ cup chopped fresh basil

4 cloves garlic, minced

¼ teaspoon cayenne pepper

10-ounce package frozen chopped spinach, thawed and squeezed dry

1 large tomato, halved, seeded, and coarsely chopped

1 cup grated Parmesan cheese

2 tablespoons pine nuts

3 ounces part-skim mozzarella cheese, shredded (about ¾ cup)

2 tablespoons plain dried bread crumbs

1. In a large pot of boiling water, cook the bell pepper until just crisp-tender, about 2 minutes. Reserve the boiling water for the ruote and, with a slotted spoon, transfer the pepper to a colander to drain. Cook the ruote in the reserved boiling water until just tender. Drain well. Return the ruote and bell pepper to the cooking pot and set aside.

2. Meanwhile, preheat the oven to 375°. Place the flour in a large saucepan over medium heat, and gradually whisk in the milk. Bring to a boil and cook, whisking frequently, until the mixture is slightly thickened, about 5 minutes.

3. Whisk in the basil, garlic, and cayenne and cook until the flavors have blended, about 4 minutes longer. Remove from the heat and stir in the spinach, tomato, and Parmesan. Pour the spinach sauce over the ruote mixture and toss well to combine.

4. Spray a 2-quart baking dish with nonstick cooking spray. Spoon the ruote mixture into the prepared baking dish. Scatter the pine nuts over, cover with foil, and bake for 15 minutes, or until the casserole is piping hot. Remove the foil, sprinkle the mozzarella over, and dust with the bread crumbs. Bake for 5 minutes longer, or until the the cheese is melted and the crumbs are golden.

Suggested accompaniment: Plum halves drizzled with honey and broiled.

Fat: 15g/26%
Calories: 512
Saturated Fat: 7.5g
Carbohydrate: 65g
Protein: 31g
Cholesterol: 34mg
Sodium: 639mg

Ham and Scalloped Potatoes

Serves: 4
Working time: 25 minutes
Total time: 50 minutes

1½ pounds all-purpose potatoes, peeled and cut into ¼-inch-thick slices

3 tablespoons flour

3 cups evaporated low-fat milk

½ pound thin asparagus, tough ends trimmed, cut into 2-inch pieces

1 cup minced scallions

1 cup frozen peas, thawed

¼ teaspoon cayenne pepper

6 ounces baked ham, cut into ¼-inch dice

2 ounces Cheddar cheese, shredded (about ½ cup)

1. Preheat the oven to 400°. In a large pot of boiling water, cook the potatoes until tender, about 12 minutes. Drain well and set aside.

2. Meanwhile, place the flour in a large saucepan over medium heat, and gradually whisk in the evaporated milk. Bring to a boil and cook, whisking frequently, until the mixture is creamy and slightly thickened, about 4 minutes. Stir in the asparagus, scallions, peas, and cayenne and cook, stirring frequently, for 2 minutes longer. Remove from the heat.

3. Spray a 9 x 9-inch glass baking dish with nonstick cooking spray. Layer half of the potatoes in the prepared baking dish and sprinkle half of the ham on top. Repeat with the remaining potatoes and ham. Pour the milk mixture over, sprinkle the Cheddar on top, and bake for 20 minutes, or until the casserole is bubbly and piping hot. Divide the ham and scalloped potatoes among 4 plates and serve.

Suggested accompaniments: Thin bread sticks, and navel orange slices sprinkled with toasted coconut for dessert.

In this warming version of one of our favorite comfort foods—terrific for supper, lunch, or brunch—we've retained the usual creamy goodness but without the cream: Flour and evaporated low-fat milk are the smart stand-ins. If fresh asparagus is not available, substitute frozen spears, fresh broccoli florets cut into small pieces, or even zucchini slices.

Fat: 14g/26%
Calories: 468
Saturated Fat: 4.5g
Carbohydrate: 56g
Protein: 31g
Cholesterol: 70mg
Sodium: 897mg

TUNA-NOODLE BAKE

SERVES: 4
WORKING TIME: 25 MINUTES
TOTAL TIME: 50 MINUTES

6 ounces yolk-free egg noodles

½ cup plus 2 tablespoons skim milk

2 tablespoons flour

¾ teaspoon dry mustard

2 teaspoons olive oil

3 scallions, chopped

1 rib celery, chopped

1 red bell pepper, diced

1 cup sliced mushrooms

¼ teaspoon dried thyme

¾ cup evaporated skimmed milk

6⅛-ounce can water-packed tuna, rinsed, drained, and flaked

1½ ounces white Cheddar cheese, shredded (about ⅓ cup)

¼ teaspoon hot pepper sauce

¼ teaspoon salt

3 tablespoons low-fat wheat cracker crumbs or plain dried bread crumbs

1. Preheat the oven to 375°. In a large saucepan of boiling water, cook the noodles until just tender. Drain well and set aside.

2. Meanwhile, in a jar with a tight-fitting lid, shake together the skim milk, flour, and mustard until smooth. Set aside. In a nonstick Dutch oven, heat the oil until hot but not smoking over medium-high heat. Add the scallions, celery, bell pepper, mushrooms, and thyme and cook, stirring frequently, until the vegetables are just tender, about 8 minutes.

3. Stir in the skim milk mixture along with the evaporated milk and bring to a boil, stirring constantly. Reduce to a simmer and cook, stirring occasionally, until the mixture is slightly thickened, about 4 minutes. Remove from the heat and stir in the tuna, Cheddar, hot pepper sauce, and salt. Add the noodles and toss to combine.

4. Spray a 1½-quart baking dish with nonstick cooking spray. Spoon the tuna-noodle mixture into the prepared baking dish, sprinkle the cracker crumbs on top, and bake for 20 to 25 minutes, or until the crumbs are golden brown and the casserole is piping hot.

Suggested accompaniment: For dessert, vanilla ice milk mixed with mashed bananas and a sprinkling of chopped peanuts.

This rich, homey casserole belies its low-fat components: yolk-free egg noodles, skim milk and evaporated skimmed milk for the sauce, water-packed tuna, and crumbled low-fat wheat crackers for the topping. You may assemble the dish earlier in the day to avoid last-minute fretting, but sprinkle on the cracker crumbs just before baking.

FAT: 8G/19%
CALORIES: 364
SATURATED FAT: 3G
CARBOHYDRATE: 47G
PROTEIN: 27G
CHOLESTEROL: 30MG
SODIUM: 487MG

Cod Fillets in Parchment

SERVES: 4
WORKING TIME: 20 MINUTES
TOTAL TIME: 35 MINUTES

*L*et *each diner open his own packet to inhale the aroma of the herb-scented fish—but do discard the bay leaves before the first forkful.*

½ cup couscous

½ cup shredded zucchini

½ cup shredded carrot

¼ cup finely chopped onion

½ teaspoon grated lemon zest

½ teaspoon salt

¼ teaspoon ground allspice

¼ teaspoon ground cumin

½ cup reduced-sodium chicken broth, defatted

4 cod fillets (about 4 ounces each), any visible bones removed

⅛ teaspoon white pepper

4 small bay leaves

1 lemon, thinly sliced

2 tablespoons chopped almonds, toasted

1. Preheat the oven to 400°. Cut four 10-inch sheets of parchment paper or foil. In a medium bowl, combine the couscous, zucchini, carrot, onion, lemon zest, ¼ teaspoon of the salt, the allspice, and cumin and stir to blend.

2. Spoon one-quarter of the couscous mixture in the center of each parchment sheet and sprinkle each portion with 2 tablespoons of the broth. Place the cod on top and sprinkle with the pepper and remaining ¼ teaspoon salt, dividing evenly. Top with the bay leaves, lemon slices, and almonds, dividing evenly. Fold the parchment over the filling and crimp the edges to seal. Place the packets on a baking sheet and bake for 15 minutes, or until the cod is just opaque.

3. Place the packets on 4 plates. Cut a cross in the center of each packet, carefully pull back the paper (the mixture may steam), and serve.

Suggested accompaniments: Belgian endive and watercress salad with an oregano vinaigrette, followed by homemade applesauce sprinkled with toasted sesame seeds.

FAT: 3G/13%
CALORIES: 226
SATURATED FAT: .4G
CARBOHYDRATE: 25G
PROTEIN: 25G
CHOLESTEROL: 49MG
SODIUM: 425MG

PIES & PIZZAS

4

Chili Pie

SERVES: 4
WORKING TIME: 20 MINUTES
TOTAL TIME: 55 MINUTES

Not your ordinary mashed potatoes, the "crust" for this pie is instead a garlicky concoction made creamy with buttermilk, and flavor-zapped with chilies. And the chili powder-spiked beef mixture is further enhanced with cilantro and cumin. Extra-lean ground beef should contain about ten percent fat—check the label. Alternatively, have the butcher grind a lean cut of sirloin or round for you.

2 pounds baking potatoes, peeled and thinly sliced

3 cloves garlic, peeled

½ teaspoon salt

¾ pound extra-lean ground beef

8-ounce can no-salt-added tomato sauce

½ cup chopped fresh cilantro or parsley

¼ cup thinly sliced scallions

¼ cup dark raisins

¼ cup pitted green olives, coarsely chopped

1 tablespoon chili powder

½ teaspoon ground cumin

¼ cup low-fat (1.5%) buttermilk

4-ounce can chopped mild green chilies, drained

1 tomato, halved and thinly sliced

2 tablespoons shredded Cheddar cheese

1. In a large pot of boiling water, cook the potatoes, garlic, and ¼ teaspoon of the salt until the potatoes and garlic are tender, about 15 minutes. Drain well.

2. Meanwhile, preheat the oven to 375°. In a large bowl, combine the beef, tomato sauce, cilantro, scallions, raisins, olives, chili powder, cumin, and remaining ¼ teaspoon salt. Mix well and set aside.

3. Spray a 9-inch deep-dish pie plate with nonstick cooking spray. Transfer the potatoes and garlic to a large bowl. Add the buttermilk and mash the mixture until smooth. Fold in the chilies. Spoon the mashed potato mixture into the prepared pie plate, smoothing evenly over the bottom and up the sides.

4. Spoon the beef mixture on top of the potatoes to within 1 inch of the edges. Bake for 20 minutes, or until the beef is cooked through and the potatoes are piping hot. Arrange the tomato slices around the edges of the pie, sprinkle the cheese in the center, and bake for 5 minutes longer, or until the cheese is melted.

Suggested accompaniments: Iced herbal tea, and pear ice for dessert.

FAT: 12G/28%
CALORIES: 387
SATURATED FAT: 4.5G
CARBOHYDRATE: 48G
PROTEIN: 24G
CHOLESTEROL: 57MG
SODIUM: 789MG

SHEPHERD'S PIE

SERVES: 4
WORKING TIME: 25 MINUTES
TOTAL TIME: 55 MINUTES

The topping for this pie is a tasty mix of mashed potatoes, turnips, parsnips, and carrots, which complements the savory beef underneath.

1½ pounds baking potatoes, peeled and thinly sliced

¾ pound turnips, thinly sliced

¾ pound parsnips, thinly sliced

4 cloves garlic, peeled, plus 3 cloves garlic, minced

3 carrots, thinly sliced

¾ pound extra-lean ground beef

¾ cup minced onions

14½-ounce can no-salt-added stewed tomatoes, drained and coarsely chopped

½ cup evaporated skimmed milk

2 tablespoons no-salt-added tomato paste

¾ teaspoon salt

½ teaspoon dried sage

½ teaspoon dried rosemary

1 cup frozen peas, thawed

⅓ cup shredded Cheddar cheese

1. Preheat the oven to 400°. In a large pot of boiling water, cook the potatoes, turnips, parsnips, peeled garlic, and carrots until the vegetables are tender, about 20 minutes. Drain well.

2. Meanwhile, spray a 9-inch deep-dish pie plate with nonstick cooking spray. In a medium bowl, combine the beef, onions, minced garlic, tomatoes, ¼ cup of the evaporated milk, the tomato paste, ¼ teaspoon of the salt, the sage, and rosemary. Mix well. Stir in the peas and pat the mixture into the prepared pie plate.

3. Transfer the vegetables to a large bowl. Add the remaining ¼ cup evaporated milk and remaining ½ teaspoon salt and mash the mixture until smooth.

4. Spoon the mashed vegetables into a pastry bag fitted with a star tip (or use a sturdy plastic bag with a bottom corner snipped off). Pipe the mixture decoratively around the edges and over the top of the beef mixture. Place the pie on a baking sheet and bake for 22 minutes, or until the topping is lightly golden. Sprinkle the Cheddar over and bake for 3 minutes longer, or until the cheese is melted and the beef is cooked through.

Suggested accompaniment: For dessert, mixed stewed fruit topped with a dollop of whipped evaporated skimmed milk.

FAT: 13G/23%
CALORIES: 502
SATURATED FAT: 5.5G
CARBOHYDRATE: 70G
PROTEIN: 31G
CHOLESTEROL: 64MG
SODIUM: 725MG

Potato-Topped Turkey Pie

SERVES: 4
WORKING TIME: 30 MINUTES
TOTAL TIME: 1 HOUR 10 MINUTES

1 pound all-purpose potatoes, peeled and cubed

5 scallions, green parts minced, white parts thinly sliced

⅓ cup low-fat (1.5%) buttermilk

1 tablespoon olive oil

½ teaspoon salt

10 ounces mushrooms, sliced

2 cloves garlic, minced

2 tablespoons dry sherry

1½ teaspoons ground ginger

1 teaspoon dry mustard

¾ teaspoon rubbed sage

14½-ounce can reduced-sodium chicken broth, defatted

¾ pound turkey breast, cut into ½-inch cubes

10-ounce package frozen green beans, thawed

½ cup low-fat (1%) milk

3 tablespoons cornstarch

2 tablespoons grated Parmesan cheese

1. In a large saucepan of boiling water, cook the potatoes until tender, about 15 minutes. Drain and transfer to a large bowl. Add the scallion greens, buttermilk, oil, and ¼ teaspoon of the salt and mash the mixture until smooth.

2. Meanwhile, preheat the oven to 400°. In a large saucepan, combine the scallion whites, mushrooms, garlic, sherry, ginger, mustard, and sage. Bring to a simmer over medium-low heat and cook until the liquid is almost evaporated, about 8 minutes. Stir in the broth, turkey, green beans, and remaining ¼ teaspoon salt. Cook until the beans are almost tender, about 5 minutes longer. Increase the heat to medium-high and bring the mixture to a boil.

3. In a cup, combine the milk and cornstarch, stir to blend, and stir into the boiling turkey mixture. Cook, stirring constantly, until the mixture is slightly thickened, about 1 minute. Spoon the turkey mixture into a 10-inch deep-dish pie plate, then spoon the mashed potatoes on top, leaving an open center. Sprinkle the Parmesan over the potatoes, place the pie on a baking sheet, and bake for 25 minutes, or until the pie is piping hot.

Suggested accompaniment: Warm buttermilk biscuits.

FAT: 6G/17%
CALORIES: 322
SATURATED FAT: 1.6G
CARBOHYDRATE: 36G
PROTEIN: 30G
CHOLESTEROL: 57MG
SODIUM: 684MG

A touch of sherry adds an alluring flavor to the homey filling, but chicken broth could easily be substituted.

GREEK SPINACH AND FETA PIE

SERVES: 4
WORKING TIME: 30 MINUTES
TOTAL TIME: 1 HOUR 5 MINUTES

1 cup low-fat (1%) cottage cheese

½ cup low-fat (1%) milk

2 tablespoons flour

2 egg whites

8 ounces baking potato, peeled and grated

2 cups diced yellow summer squash

2 cloves garlic, minced

⅓ cup reduced-sodium chicken broth, defatted

10-ounce package frozen chopped spinach, thawed and squeezed dry

½ cup minced scallions

½ cup chopped fresh mint

½ teaspoon dried oregano

¼ teaspoon grated lemon zest

¼ teaspoon salt

¼ teaspoon ground black pepper

Six 17 x 11-inch sheets phyllo dough, thawed if frozen

2 ounces feta cheese, crumbled

1. Preheat the oven to 350°. In a food processor or blender, purée the cottage cheese, milk, flour, and egg whites until smooth. Set aside.

2. Spray a large nonstick skillet with nonstick cooking spray, then place over medium heat. Add the potato, squash, garlic, and broth and cook, stirring frequently, until the potato and squash are tender and the liquid is absorbed, about 5 minutes. Stir in the spinach, scallions, and mint and cook until the spinach is heated through, about 2 minutes longer. Remove from the heat and stir in the oregano, lemon zest, salt, and pepper. Set aside.

3. Spray a 9-inch deep-dish pie plate with nonstick cooking spray. One at a time, layer the phyllo sheets in the prepared pie plate, lightly spraying each sheet with nonstick cooking spray, overlapping the sheets at right angles, and letting the edges overhang the sides by about 2 inches. Spoon the spinach mixture over the phyllo, pour the cottage cheese purée over, and sprinkle the feta on top. Lightly spray the phyllo overhang with nonstick cooking spray and fold the overhang loosely over the filling, leaving the center open. Bake for 35 minutes, or until the phyllo is lightly golden.

Suggested accompaniments: Cucumber and dill salad, and wedges of honeydew melon with a squeeze of lime to finish.

FAT: 8G/26%
CALORIES: 286
SATURATED FAT: 3G
CARBOHYDRATE: 37G
PROTEIN: 18G
CHOLESTEROL: 16MG
SODIUM: 815MG

Crispy phyllo pastry is much used in Greek cooking. You can usually find it in the frozen foods case in your supermarket. Rather than slathering the layers with oil or butter as is typically done, we spritz them with nonstick cooking spray, keeping fat to a minimum. Feta is a soft, crumbly, cured Greek cheese, and it can be recognized by its salty, tangy flavor— a little goes a long way.

This
veritable garden of
vegetables is generously
seasoned with tarragon
and topped with a
Cheddar crust. The
dough may be crumbly
when patting into the
round, but don't
worry—just pinch
and pat it together
again as needed.
Try substituting
different vegetables as
the season warrants.

VEGETABLE POT PIE

SERVES: 4
WORKING TIME: 30 MINUTES
TOTAL TIME: 50 MINUTES

6 ounces all-purpose potato, peeled and cut into ¼-inch dice

1 teaspoon plus 2 tablespoons olive oil

1 medium onion, cut into ½-inch chunks

3 cloves garlic, minced

2 red bell peppers, diced

2 zucchini, halved lengthwise and cut into ½-inch-thick slices

2 carrots, halved lengthwise and cut into ¼-inch-thick slices

1½ cups quartered mushrooms

Two 14½-ounce cans no-salt-added stewed tomatoes, drained and chopped

1 teaspoon dried tarragon

¾ teaspoon salt

1½ cups flour

2 ounces sharp Cheddar cheese, shredded (about ½ cup)

1½ teaspoons baking powder

½ teaspoon baking soda

1 cup low-fat (1.5%) buttermilk

1. In a medium saucepan of boiling water, cook the potato until tender, about 15 minutes. Drain well and set aside.

2. Meanwhile, spray a nonstick Dutch oven with nonstick cooking spray, add 1 teaspoon of the oil, and heat until hot but not smoking over medium heat. Add the onion and garlic and cook, stirring frequently, until the onion is softened, about 7 minutes. Add the bell peppers, zucchini, carrots, and mushrooms, stirring to coat. Add the tomatoes, tarragon, and ½ teaspoon of the salt. Bring to a boil, reduce to a simmer, cover, and cook until the peppers and carrots are crisp-tender, about 7 minutes. Stir in the potato and spoon the mixture into a 9-inch deep-dish pie plate.

3. Preheat the oven to 375°. In a large bowl, stir together the flour, cheese, baking powder, baking soda, and remaining ¼ teaspoon salt. In a small bowl, stir together the buttermilk and remaining 2 tablespoons oil. Make a well in the center of the flour mixture, add the buttermilk mixture, and stir just until a dough forms.

4. On a lightly floured board, gently knead the dough and pat into an 8-inch round. Place the dough over the vegetable mixture (see tip; top photo) and score the dough about ¼ inch deep (bottom photo). Place the pie on a baking sheet and bake for 17 minutes, or until the crust is golden and the filling is piping hot.

Suggested accompaniment: Reduced-calorie lemon pudding with berries.

FAT: 15G/28%
CALORIES: 471
SATURATED FAT: 4.8G
CARBOHYDRATE: 73G
PROTEIN: 16G
CHOLESTEROL: 19MG
SODIUM: 928MG

TIP

Center the dough over the vegetable filling. For a decorative finishing touch, with a sharp paring knife, score the dough in a lattice pattern about ¼ inch deep, being careful not to cut all the way through the dough. However, don't score too lightly or the design won't show up.

A
little part-skim ricotta mixed with full-flavored Parmesan creates the illusion of richness in this infinitely appealing vegetable pizza. For a really authentic pie, ask your local pizza parlor if you can purchase some of their dough. Also, many supermarkets have good-quality ready-to-use pizza dough.

RUSTIC PIZZA

SERVES: 4
WORKING TIME: 25 MINUTES
TOTAL TIME: 50 MINUTES

2 teaspoons olive oil

1 medium onion, halved and thinly sliced

4 cloves garlic, slivered

2 red bell peppers, cut into thin strips

2 yellow summer squash, thinly sliced

1 cup no-salt-added tomato sauce

½ cup chopped fresh basil

¼ cup orange juice

10-ounce package all-ready pizza crust

1 cup part-skim ricotta cheese

¼ cup plus 1 tablespoon grated Parmesan cheese

½ teaspoon freshly ground black pepper

¼ teaspoon salt

2 egg whites

1. In a large skillet, heat the oil until hot but not smoking over medium heat. Add the onion and garlic and cook, stirring frequently, until the onion is golden, about 7 minutes. Add the bell peppers and squash, stirring to coat. Add the tomato sauce, basil, and orange juice and bring to a simmer. Cook, stirring occasionally, until the mixture has thickened, about 9 minutes. Cool to room temperature. Drain and discard any liquid.

2. Meanwhile, preheat the oven to 425° with the rack on the lowest shelf. On a nonstick baking sheet, unroll the pizza crust and press into a 12-inch square. In a medium bowl, stir together the ricotta, ¼ cup of the Parmesan, the black pepper, salt, and 1 of the egg whites. Spread the ricotta mixture evenly over the crust to within 2 inches of the edges.

3. Spoon the vegetable sauce over the ricotta mixture. Fold over the crust edges, making square corners (see tip; top photo). Brush the crust with the remaining 1 egg white (bottom photo) and sprinkle with the remaining 1 tablespoon Parmesan. Bake on the lowest oven rack for 14 minutes, or until the crust is golden and the pizza is piping hot. Cut the pizza into quarters and serve.

Suggested accompaniments: Spinach salad with a garlic vinaigrette. For dessert, fresh cherries served with chocolate syrup for dipping.

FAT: 12G/27%
CALORIES: 412
SATURATED FAT: 5.1G
CARBOHYDRATE: 54G
PROTEIN: 20G
CHOLESTEROL: 24MG
SODIUM: 763MG

TIP

After arranging the filling on the dough, leaving a 2-inch border all around, fold the dough over the filling, making the corners square. Brush the dough lightly with egg white before adding the Parmesan so that it will adhere.

GROUND BEEF PASTIES WITH CHUTNEY SAUCE

SERVES: 4
WORKING TIME: 35 MINUTES
TOTAL TIME: 1 HOUR 50 MINUTES (INCLUDES CHILLING)

1¼ cups flour

½ cup yellow cornmeal

1 teaspoon sugar

1 teaspoon paprika

½ teaspoon salt

⅛ teaspoon cayenne pepper

4 tablespoons reduced-fat cream cheese (Neufchâtel)

1 cup plain nonfat yogurt

1 large onion, halved and thinly sliced

1 red bell pepper, cut into thin strips

1 green bell pepper, cut into thin strips

4 cloves garlic, minced

⅓ cup reduced-sodium chicken broth, defatted

¾ pound extra-lean ground beef

4 tablespoons prepared chutney

1 teaspoon ground ginger

¾ teaspoon cinnamon

½ teaspoon freshly ground black pepper

1 teaspoon cornstarch

1. In a large bowl, combine the flour, cornmeal, sugar, paprika, ¼ teaspoon of the salt, and the cayenne. With a pastry blender or 2 knives, cut in the cream cheese until coarse crumbs form. Stir in ¾ cup of the yogurt just until a dough forms. Chill for 1 hour.

2. Meanwhile, spray a large nonstick skillet with nonstick cooking spray, then place over medium heat. Add the onion and cook, stirring frequently, until softened, about 5 minutes. Add the bell peppers, garlic, and broth, cover, and cook for 10 minutes. Stir in the beef, 3 tablespoons of the chutney, the ginger, cinnamon, black pepper, and remaining ¼ teaspoon salt and cook, uncovered, until the beef is browned, about 5 minutes. In a cup, combine the cornstarch and 2 teaspoons of water, stir to blend, and stir into the beef mixture. Bring to a boil and cook, stirring, for 1 minute. Set aside.

3. Preheat the oven to 375°. Spray 2 baking sheets with nonstick cooking spray. Divide the dough into 4 pieces. On a lightly floured board, roll each piece into a 9-inch round and place on the prepared baking sheets. Spoon one-quarter of the beef mixture into the center of each round, brush edges with water, fold in half, and crimp the edges. Prick the tops with a fork and bake for 15 minutes, or until golden. In a small bowl, stir together the remaining ¼ cup yogurt and 1 tablespoon chutney. Serve with the pasties.

Suggested accompaniment: Mixed salad with a parsley vinaigrette.

FAT: 14G/24%
CALORIES: 515
SATURATED FAT: 5.7G
CARBOHYDRATE: 70G
PROTEIN: 29G
CHOLESTEROL: 65MG
SODIUM: 526MG

Earlier versions of these hand-held treats were traditional lunch fare for tin miners in Cornwall, England. We've used reduced-fat cream cheese and nonfat yogurt in the dough for a richer crust without excessive fat, and added cornmeal for texture. And the beef filling is piquantly seasoned with chutney, ginger, and cinnamon. For convenience, you can chill the dough overnight.

*T*his inviting beef pie gets a boost of flavor and subtle sweetness from root vegetables, deliciously scented with basil, oregano, and thyme. Using frozen pearl onions eliminates all the fuss of peeling fresh. To keep the fat in the crust in check, we lightly oil the phyllo layers and sprinkle them with bread crumbs.

Beef Pot Pie in Phyllo

SERVES: 4
WORKING TIME: 30 MINUTES
TOTAL TIME: 1 HOUR 5 MINUTES

10 ounces lean bottom round of beef, cut into ¼-inch cubes

14½-ounce can reduced-sodium beef broth, defatted

1 cup frozen pearl onions, thawed

1 cup sliced carrots

1 cup quartered and sliced parsnips

1 cup diced red potatoes

½ teaspoon dried basil

½ teaspoon dried oregano

¼ teaspoon dried thyme

¼ teaspoon salt

½ cup low-fat (1%) milk

⅓ cup flour

1 cup frozen peas, thawed

⅛ teaspoon freshly ground black pepper

Four 17 x 11-inch sheets phyllo dough, thawed if frozen

1½ tablespoons olive oil

2 tablespoons plain dried bread crumbs

1. In a large saucepan, combine the beef and broth. Bring to a boil over high heat, reduce to a simmer, cover, and cook for 15 minutes. Stir in the onions, carrots, parsnips, potatoes, basil, oregano, thyme, and salt. Return to a boil, reduce to a simmer, cover again, and cook until the vegetables are almost tender, about 10 minutes.

2. Preheat the oven to 375°. In a jar with a tight-fitting lid, combine the milk and flour, shake until smooth, and stir into the simmering beef mixture. Cook, uncovered, stirring constantly, until the vegetables are tender and the mixture is slightly thickened, about 5 minutes longer. Stir in the peas and pepper and spoon the mixture into an 11 x 7-inch baking dish.

3. Lightly brush one phyllo sheet with some of the oil, then sprinkle with some of the bread crumbs (see tip; top photo). Place a second phyllo sheet on top, then brush with more oil and sprinkle with more bread crumbs. Repeat with the remaining phyllo, oil, and bread crumbs. Cut the stack crosswise into 1½-inch-wide strips (middle photo). Arrange the strips diagonally over the beef mixture, trimming the ends to fit and tucking the scraps under the strips to use up (bottom photo). Bake for 25 minutes, or until the phyllo is crisp and lightly golden and the filling is piping hot.

Suggested accompaniments: Crusty rolls. For dessert, tapioca pudding topped with mandarin orange sections.

FAT: 11G/26%
CALORIES: 388
SATURATED FAT: 2.5G
CARBOHYDRATE: 47G
PROTEIN: 24G
CHOLESTEROL: 43MG
SODIUM: 651MG

PORK AND APPLE POT PIE

SERVES: 4
WORKING TIME: 35 MINUTES
TOTAL TIME: 1 HOUR 10 MINUTES

We've topped this country pie with squares of golden-brown pastry, sensibly enriched with reduced-fat cream cheese and nonfat yogurt. For more low-fat finesse, we've used just two ounces of lean ground pork per serving, and stretched it with pinto beans—white beans would work as well. Both the filling and the dough can be made a day ahead and refrigerated separately.

2 teaspoons olive oil
2 medium red onions, chopped
½ pound lean ground pork
1 cup diced Granny Smith apple
1 cup sliced carrots
1 cup diced turnip
1 cup canned pinto beans, rinsed and drained
¾ teaspoon poultry seasoning or dried sage
¼ teaspoon dried thyme
3 tablespoons plus 1¾ cups flour
¼ cup reduced-fat sour cream
⅛ teaspoon black pepper
2 tablespoons cold reduced-fat cream cheese (Neufchâtel)
1 tablespoon cold unsalted butter
2 teaspoons baking powder
1 teaspoon baking soda
¼ teaspoon salt
1 cup plain nonfat yogurt

1. In a large nonstick saucepan, heat the oil until hot but not smoking over medium heat. Add the onions and cook, stirring frequently, until the onions are softened, about 7 minutes. Add the pork and cook, stirring, until browned, about 5 minutes. Drain off the fat. Stir in the apple, carrots, turnip, beans, ¾ cup of water, poultry seasoning, and thyme. Bring to a boil, reduce to a simmer, cover, and cook until the carrots and turnip are just tender, about 12 minutes.

2. Preheat the oven to 400°. In a cup, combine the 3 tablespoons flour and 5 tablespoons of water, stir until smooth, and stir into the simmering pork mixture. Cook, uncovered, stirring constantly, until the mixture is slightly thickened, about 2 minutes longer. Remove from the heat, stir in the sour cream and pepper, and spoon the mixture into a 9-inch deep-dish pie plate.

3. In a food processor, combine the remaining 1¾ cups flour, the cream cheese, butter, baking powder, baking soda, and salt and process until coarse crumbs form. Add the yogurt and pulse with on/off turns just until combined. On a lightly floured board, pat the dough into an 8-inch square about ¼ inch thick. Cut into sixteen 2-inch squares, arrange on top of the pork mixture, and place the pie on a baking sheet. Bake for 20 minutes, or until the squares are lightly golden and the filling is piping hot.

Suggested accompaniment: Broiled peach halves with maple syrup.

FAT: 15G/24%
CALORIES: 550
SATURATED FAT: 5.9G
CARBOHYDRATE: 77G
PROTEIN: 28G
CHOLESTEROL: 57MG
SODIUM: 981MG

This loaf is a spectacular version of a ham and cheese sandwich: Layers of mozzarella, ham, and spinach are highlighted with a garlicky tomato sauce. Using ready-to-go frozen bread dough makes the assembly especially convenient. The dough may be difficult to roll at first, but if you keep gently rolling it will soon reach the proper size.

STROMBOLI

SERVES: 4
WORKING TIME: 35 MINUTES
TOTAL TIME: 55 MINUTES

2 teaspoons olive oil

2 large onions, halved and thinly sliced

4 cloves garlic, slivered

1 cup chopped fresh tomato

3 tablespoons no-salt-added tomato paste

2 teaspoons red wine vinegar

½ teaspoon dried thyme

¼ teaspoon freshly ground black pepper

1 pound frozen bread dough, thawed

2 tablespoons plain dried bread crumbs

2 ounces thinly sliced reduced-sodium ham

4 ounces part-skim mozzarella cheese, shredded (about 1 cup)

10-ounce package frozen chopped spinach, thawed and squeezed dry

1 cup rinsed, drained, and diced jarred roasted red peppers

¼ cup chopped fresh basil

2 tablespoons grated Parmesan cheese

1. Spray a large nonstick skillet with nonstick cooking spray. Add 1 teaspoon of the oil, then place over medium heat. Add the onions and garlic and cook, stirring frequently, until the onions are softened, about 5 minutes. Stir in the tomato, tomato paste, vinegar, thyme, and black pepper and cook until the mixture is slightly thickened, about 7 minutes longer. Remove from the heat. Set aside.

2. Preheat the oven to 400°. On a lightly floured board, roll the bread dough into a 15 x 12-inch rectangle. Sprinkle the bread crumbs over. Spoon the onion mixture on top of the dough to within ½ inch of the edges, lay the ham over the onions in a single layer, and sprinkle the mozzarella on top. In a small bowl, stir together the spinach, red peppers, and basil and scatter the mixture over the mozzarella.

3. Spray a baking sheet with nonstick cooking spray. Starting at one long side, roll up the dough, jelly-roll style (see tip; top photo). Pinch the seam (middle photo) and the ends (bottom photo) to seal. Place the roll, seam-side down, on the prepared baking sheet. Brush the top with the remaining 1 teaspoon oil and sprinkle with the Parmesan. Cut several slashes in the top to release steam and bake for 20 minutes, or until the stromboli is lightly golden and the filling is piping hot.

Suggested accompaniment: Assorted fresh fruit for dessert.

FAT: 12G/21%
CALORIES: 505
SATURATED FAT: 3.9G
CARBOHYDRATE: 78G
PROTEIN: 24G
CHOLESTEROL: 25MG
SODIUM: 1,125MG

MEXICAN-STYLE PIZZA

SERVES: 4
WORKING TIME: 10 MINUTES
TOTAL TIME: 25 MINUTES

Ten 6-inch corn tortillas

4 ounces Monterey jack cheese, shredded (about 1 cup)

1¾ cups canned black beans, rinsed and drained

2 tablespoons fresh lime juice

½ teaspoon ground coriander

½ teaspoon dried oregano

½ cup minced scallions

½ cup chopped fresh cilantro

1 green bell pepper, cut into thin strips

2 plum tomatoes, thinly sliced

1. Preheat the oven to 400°. Spray a baking sheet with nonstick cooking spray. Arrange the tortillas in a circle on the prepared baking sheet, overlapping them slightly. Sprinkle ¾ cup of the cheese on top. Set aside.

2. In a medium bowl, stir together the beans, lime juice, 1 tablespoon of water, the coriander, and oregano. With a potato masher or the back of a spoon, mash the mixture until smooth. Add the scallions and cilantro and stir well to combine.

3. Spread the bean mixture over the cheese on the tortillas. Scatter half of the bell pepper over, arrange the tomatoes on top, and scatter the remaining pepper over. Sprinkle the remaining ¼ cup cheese on top and bake for 10 minutes, or until the tortillas are crisp and the cheese is melted.

Suggested accompaniments: Lemonade, and a green salad with chopped black olives drizzled with a citrus vinaigrette. Follow with fat-free pound cake slices topped with warm apricot jam.

This eye-catching pizza takes practically no time to assemble since the crust is simply corn tortillas. You just layer on the cheese, black beans, and other flavorful ingredients. The meaty plum tomatoes hold their shape particularly well during the baking. To serve, cut the pizza into wedges with kitchen scissors or a pizza wheel cutter.

FAT: 11G/29%
CALORIES: 341
SATURATED FAT: 5.3G
CARBOHYDRATE: 46G
PROTEIN: 16G
CHOLESTEROL: 30MG
SODIUM: 485MG

Can a quiche really be low-fat? Here's how—instead of a fat-laden pastry, we use a rice-based "crust." For the filling, we use just two whole eggs with extra whites, and then add nonfat yogurt and skim milk to create a creamy custard. Reduced-fat Cheddar adds tang, and a small amount of Canadian bacon lends just enough smoky flavor.

RICE-CRUSTED QUICHE LORRAINE

SERVES: 4
WORKING TIME: 25 MINUTES
TOTAL TIME: 1 HOUR 30 MINUTES

1½ cups long-grain rice

1 small onion, finely chopped

¼ teaspoon salt

3 tablespoons grated Parmesan cheese

2 eggs

3 egg whites, plus 2 egg whites, lightly beaten

1 cup skim milk

1 cup plain nonfat yogurt

1 teaspoon dry mustard

½ cup chopped fresh parsley

2 ounces Canadian bacon, diced

2 ounces reduced-fat Cheddar cheese, shredded (about ½ cup)

½ cup diced red bell pepper

1. In a large saucepan, combine the rice, onion, salt, and 3 cups of water. Bring to a boil over high heat, reduce to a simmer, cover, and cook for 12 minutes. Remove from the heat and let stand, covered, until the liquid is absorbed, about 5 minutes.

2. Meanwhile, preheat the oven to 350°. Spray a 9-inch quiche dish or deep-dish pie plate with nonstick cooking spray.

3. Sprinkle the Parmesan over the prepared dish, tilting to coat the bottom and sides. Tap out the excess Parmesan onto a sheet of waxed paper, then transfer to a blender or food processor. Add the eggs, the 3 egg whites, milk, yogurt, and mustard and purée the mixture until smooth. Set aside.

4. Stir the parsley and remaining 2 egg whites into the rice mixture until well combined. Spoon the mixture into the Parmesan-coated dish, pressing evenly over the bottom and up the sides (see tip). Sprinkle the bacon, Cheddar, and bell pepper on top. Pour the milk mixture over and bake for 45 to 55 minutes, or until the top is golden brown and a knife inserted near the center comes out clean. Let stand for 15 minutes before cutting into wedges.

Suggested accompaniments: Sliced tomatoes with a basil vinaigrette. For dessert, orange sherbet sprinkled with chopped crystallized ginger.

TIP

To form the crust, spoon the herbed, cooked rice mixture evenly into the pie plate. With your fingers, firmly press the mixture evenly over the bottom of the dish and up the sides.

FAT: 8G/16%
CALORIES: 463
SATURATED FAT: 3.8G
CARBOHYDRATE: 68G
PROTEIN: 27G
CHOLESTEROL: 129MG
SODIUM: 697MG

DEEP-DISH PAN PIZZA

SERVES: 4
WORKING TIME: 25 MINUTES
TOTAL TIME: 45 MINUTES

For our version of the Chicago favorite, we pre-bake the crust, line it with a thin layer of pepperoni, and toss on lots of vegetables flavored with balsamic vinegar, rosemary, and black pepper. We top it all off with plenty of part-skim mozzarella for traditional taste. If you don't have an ovenproof skillet, wrap the handle of a regular skillet in foil.

1 pound frozen bread dough, thawed
¾ teaspoon dried rosemary
¾ teaspoon freshly ground black pepper
2 zucchini, halved lengthwise and cut into thin slices
1 medium red onion, diced
1 cup diced red bell pepper
¼ cup balsamic vinegar
2 tablespoons no-salt-added tomato paste
2 ounces thinly sliced pepperoni
1½ cups halved cherry tomatoes
4 ounces part-skim mozzarella cheese, shredded (about 1 cup)

1. Preheat the oven to 425°. Spray a large ovenproof skillet with nonstick cooking spray. On a lightly floured board, roll the bread dough into a 12-inch round. Place the dough in the prepared skillet, pressing evenly over the bottom and up the sides. Press ¼ teaspoon of the rosemary and ¼ teaspoon of the black pepper into the dough, place the pan in the oven, and bake for 15 minutes, or until the crust is lightly browned.

2. Meanwhile, spray a large nonstick skillet with nonstick cooking spray, then place over medium heat. Add the zucchini, onion, and bell pepper and cook, stirring frequently, until the onion and pepper are crisp-tender, about 4 minutes. Stir in the vinegar, tomato paste, remaining ½ teaspoon rosemary, and remaining ½ teaspoon black pepper and cook until the mixture is slightly thickened, about 4 minutes. Remove from the heat.

3. Scatter the pepperoni over the crust, spoon the zucchini mixture over, and arrange the tomatoes on top. Bake for 10 minutes, or until the topping is piping hot and the tomatoes are softened. Sprinkle the mozzarella over and bake for 3 minutes longer, or until the cheese is just melted. Serve from the pan.

Suggested accompaniments: Hearts of romaine lettuce with a nonfat ranch dressing, and reduced-fat chocolate chip ice cream for dessert.

FAT: 14G/28%
CALORIES: 456
SATURATED FAT: 5.2G
CARBOHYDRATE: 63G
PROTEIN: 21G
CHOLESTEROL: 28MG
SODIUM: 1,097MG

TAMALE PIE

SERVES: 4
WORKING TIME: 20 MINUTES
TOTAL TIME: 55 MINUTES

This festive pie features a lean ground turkey-salsa filling in a cornmeal crust, which gets an added kick from zippy spices.

¼ teaspoon salt

1 cup reduced-sodium chicken broth, defatted

¾ cup yellow cornmeal

2 teaspoons mild chili powder

1 teaspoon ground cumin

1 teaspoon dried oregano

¾ pound lean ground turkey

1½ cups mild or medium-hot chunky prepared low-sodium salsa

1 cup frozen corn kernels, thawed

2 tablespoons tomato paste

2 tablespoons chopped fresh parsley

1. Preheat the oven to 400°. Spray a 9-inch pie plate with nonstick cooking spray. In a large pot, bring 1 cup of water and the salt to a boil.

2. Meanwhile, in a medium bowl, combine the broth and cornmeal and stir well to blend. Add the cornmeal mixture to the boiling water, stirring constantly. Stir in 1 teaspoon of the chili powder, ½ teaspoon of the cumin, and ½ teaspoon of the oregano. Cook, stirring constantly, until the mixture is thickened and leaves the sides of the pot, about 5 minutes.

3. Spoon the cornmeal mixture into the prepared pie plate, smoothing evenly over the bottom and up the sides. Bake for 10 minutes, or until the crust is set. Transfer to a wire rack and cool slightly.

4. Meanwhile, in a large bowl, combine the turkey, salsa, corn, tomato paste, remaining 1 teaspoon chili powder, remaining ½ teaspoon cumin, and remaining ½ teaspoon oregano. Mix well. Spoon the turkey mixture into the crust and bake for 25 minutes, or until the crust is lightly golden and the turkey is cooked through. Sprinkle the parsley over the top and serve.

Suggested accompaniments: Boston or Bibb lettuce salad sprinkled with a little Parmesan cheese, and grapefruit slices broiled with brown sugar and cinnamon afterward.

FAT: 8G/24%
CALORIES: 288
SATURATED FAT: 1.8G
CARBOHYDRATE: 36G
PROTEIN: 20G
CHOLESTEROL: 62MG
SODIUM: 462MG

COOKING FOR A CROWD
5

Barbecue-Sauced Steak with Vegetable Kebabs

Serves: 8
Working time: 30 minutes
Total time: 1 hour 15 minutes

2 cloves garlic, peeled

Two 8-ounce cans tomato sauce

3 tablespoons tomato paste

3 tablespoons Worcestershire sauce

3 tablespoons firmly packed dark brown sugar

2 tablespoons cider vinegar

1 tablespoon chili powder

1 teaspoon dry mustard

½ teaspoon salt

¼ teaspoon cayenne pepper

1½ pounds flank steak, trimmed

3 acorn squash, halved, seeded, and cut into 2-inch pieces

3 red bell peppers, each cut into 8 pieces

1. In a blender or food processor, purée the garlic, tomato sauce, tomato paste, Worcestershire sauce, brown sugar, vinegar, chili powder, mustard, salt, and cayenne until smooth. Transfer 1 cup of the sauce to a shallow glass dish and add the steak, turning to coat. Cover and refrigerate the steak while you prepare the vegetables. Set aside the remaining sauce.

2. In a large pot of boiling water, cook the squash until just tender, about 20 minutes. Drain well and set aside to cool. Meanwhile, preheat the broiler or prepare the grill. Alternately thread the squash and bell peppers on 8 metal skewers and set aside.

3. Place the steak on the broiler or grill rack, discarding the sauce in the dish, and brush with some of the reserved sauce. Broil or grill 4 inches from the heat for 4 to 6 minutes per side for medium, or until desired doneness. Transfer the steak to a serving platter and let stand while you cook the vegetables.

4. Brush the vegetables with some more of the sauce and broil or grill for 4 to 6 minutes per side, or until the vegetables are lightly glazed. Cut the steak into thin diagonal slices, spoon the remaining sauce on top, and serve with the vegetable kebabs.

Suggested accompaniment: A hollowed-out watermelon half filled with assorted melon balls and sprinkled with lime juice and chopped mint.

Fat: 7g/26%
Calories: 245
Saturated Fat: 2.8g
Carbohydrate: 28g
Protein: 20g
Cholesterol: 43mg
Sodium: 659mg

Herald the grilling season with an American classic—this juicy flank steak dinner. Our easy barbecue sauce does double duty for the steak and vegetables. For even more flavor, marinate the meat in the refrigerator overnight. And to save time, cook the squash a day ahead. An advantage of this meal is that it will wait for your guests—it's equally good at room (or patio) temperature.

THREE-BEAN VEGETABLE CHILI

SERVES: 8
WORKING TIME: 25 MINUTES
TOTAL TIME: 55 MINUTES

This chili is so richly satisfying, don't be surprised if the gang doesn't miss the meat. We've kept the oil to a minimum, and to reduce the sodium content, we've rinsed the beans and used no-salt-added tomato products. Butternut squash is at its peak from early fall through the winter—choose squash that feels heavy for its size, with unblemished skin.

1½ tablespoons olive oil
3 large onions, diced
8 cloves garlic, slivered
2 red bell peppers, diced
6 carrots, thinly sliced
4 cups peeled, seeded, and cut butternut squash (1-inch chunks)
2 tablespoons mild or medium-hot chili powder
1 tablespoon ground coriander
2 teaspoons ground cumin
1½ teaspoons ground ginger
½ teaspoon salt
Two 14½-ounce cans no-salt-added stewed tomatoes, chopped with their juices
Two 6-ounce cans no-salt-added tomato paste
Two 19-ounce cans black beans, rinsed and drained
Two 19-ounce cans chick-peas, rinsed and drained
Two 19-ounce cans red kidney beans, rinsed and drained

1. In a large Dutch oven, heat the oil until hot but not smoking over medium heat. Add the onions and garlic and cook, stirring frequently, until the onions are golden brown, about 10 minutes.

2. Add the bell peppers and cook until the peppers are tender, about 5 minutes. Add the carrots and squash, stirring to coat. Stir in the chili powder, coriander, cumin, ginger, and salt. Cover and cook until the carrots and squash are crisp-tender, about 10 minutes.

3. Stir in the tomatoes with their juices, the tomato paste, and 1 cup of water and bring to a boil. Reduce to a simmer, cover again, and cook until the mixture is slightly thickened, about 5 minutes. Stir in the black beans, chick-peas, and kidney beans and cook, uncovered, until the flavors have blended and the beans are heated through, about 5 minutes longer.

Suggested accompaniments: Peasant bread, and a tossed salad with honey-mustard dressing. For dessert, warm apple crumble topped with reduced-fat granola.

FAT: 7G/14%
CALORIES: 452
SATURATED FAT: .6G
CARBOHYDRATE: 80G
PROTEIN: 22G
CHOLESTEROL: 0MG
SODIUM: 761MG

Just a small amount of ham adds meaty flavor to the rich yet very low-fat cottage cheese-based filling, which is sparked with jarred roasted red peppers. The manicotti can be filled earlier in the day and refrigerated. Just before baking, stir together the sauce ingredients and spoon over the manicotti in the baking dish.

Stuffed Manicotti with Ham and Cheese

SERVES: 8
WORKING TIME: 25 MINUTES
TOTAL TIME: 50 MINUTES

16 manicotti shells

7-ounce jar roasted red peppers, rinsed and drained

⅓ cup fresh parsley leaves

2 scallions, cut into 1-inch pieces

1½ cups low-fat (1%) cottage cheese

1 cup frozen peas, thawed

¾ cup finely chopped reduced-sodium baked ham

⅓ cup diced Provolone cheese, plus ⅔ cup thin strips Provolone cheese

14½-ounce can no-salt-added stewed tomatoes, chopped with their juices

½ cup chopped fresh basil

¼ cup no-salt-added tomato paste

½ teaspoon dried oregano

⅛ teaspoon hot pepper sauce

1. Spray two 11 x 7-inch baking dishes with nonstick cooking spray. In a large pot of boiling water, cook the manicotti until almost tender. Drain, rinse under cold water, and drain again. Set aside.

2. Meanwhile, preheat the oven to 400°. In a blender or food processor, purée the roasted peppers, parsley, and scallions until smooth. Scrape the purée into a large bowl and stir in the cottage cheese, peas, ham, and diced Provolone. Spoon the mixture into a sturdy plastic bag and snip off a bottom corner (see tip; top photo). Pipe the mixture into the manicotti (bottom photo) and place the shells in the prepared baking dishes.

3. In a small bowl, stir together the tomatoes with their juices, basil, tomato paste, oregano, and hot pepper sauce and spoon the mixture over the manicotti. Cover with foil and bake for 25 minutes, or until the manicotti is piping hot. Remove the foil, sprinkle the Provolone strips on top, and bake for 3 minutes longer, or until the cheese is melted. Divide the stuffed manicotti among 8 plates and serve.

Suggested accompaniments: Arugula and cherry tomato salad with a nonfat Italian dressing. Follow with sliced fresh pears drizzled with chocolate sauce.

FAT: 6G/20%
CALORIES: 250
SATURATED FAT: 2.9G
CARBOHYDRATE: 33G
PROTEIN: 17G
CHOLESTEROL: 18MG
SODIUM: 499MG

TIP

Spoon the cheese mixture into a large plastic food-storage bag. Pack the filling into the bag, twist the top of the bag closed, and snip off a bottom corner. Squeezing the top and sides of the bag, pipe the filling into each end of the manicotti, making sure to fill the shell completely.

GREEN CHILI WITH PORK

SERVES: 8
WORKING TIME: 30 MINUTES
TOTAL TIME: 50 MINUTES

This recipe is a delicious change of pace from the expected ground beef chili—lean, tender pork loin makes it lower in fat.

¼ cup flour

½ teaspoon salt

½ teaspoon freshly ground black pepper

1¼ pounds lean pork loin, cut into ½-inch chunks

2 teaspoons olive oil

2 cups thinly sliced scallions

6 cloves garlic, slivered

3 green bell peppers, diced

2 teaspoons minced pickled jalapeño pepper

Two 4-ounce cans chopped mild green chilies

2 cups reduced-sodium chicken broth, defatted

12-ounce can no-salt-added tomato paste

1 teaspoon dried oregano

Three 16-ounce cans white kidney beans (cannellini), rinsed and drained

2½ cups frozen corn kernels, thawed

½ cup chopped fresh cilantro or parsley

3 tablespoons fresh lime juice

1. On a sheet of waxed paper, combine the flour, ¼ teaspoon of the salt, and ¼ teaspoon of the black pepper. Dredge the pork in the flour mixture, shaking off the excess. In a large Dutch oven, heat the oil until hot but not smoking over medium heat. Add the pork, in batches if necessary, and cook until browned, about 5 minutes. With a slotted spoon, transfer to a plate and set aside.

2. Add the scallions and garlic to the pan and cook, stirring frequently, until the scallions are softened, about 2 minutes. Stir in the bell peppers and jalapeño and cook, stirring occasionally, until the peppers are tender, about 7 minutes.

3. Add the green chilies, stirring to coat. Stir in the broth, tomato paste, oregano, remaining ¼ teaspoon salt, and remaining ¼ teaspoon black pepper and bring to a boil. Reduce to a simmer, cover, and cook until the mixture is slightly thickened and the flavors have blended, about 10 minutes.

4. Return the pork to the pan. Stir in the beans, corn, and cilantro and cook, uncovered, until the vegetables are heated through and the pork is cooked through, about 2 minutes longer. Stir in the lime juice. Divide the chili among 8 shallow bowls and serve.

Suggested accompaniments: Red onion and orange salad with a poppy seed vinaigrette, and fat-free pound cake with raspberries for dessert.

FAT: 7G/16%
CALORIES: 357
SATURATED FAT: 1.6G
CARBOHYDRATE: 48G
PROTEIN: 30G
CHOLESTEROL: 45MG
SODIUM: 774MG

Baked Beans and Pork Chops

SERVES: 8
WORKING TIME: 35 MINUTES
TOTAL TIME: 1 HOUR 5 MINUTES

2 teaspoons olive oil

1 ounce Canadian bacon, diced

8 thin bone-in pork chops (about 4 ounces each)

3 large onions, cut into ½-inch chunks

6 cloves garlic, thinly sliced

2 tablespoons minced fresh ginger

4 carrots, halved lengthwise and cut into thin slices

2 Italian frying peppers or green bell peppers, diced

14½-ounce can no-salt-added stewed tomatoes, chopped with their juices

Four 8-ounce cans no-salt-added tomato sauce

⅓ cup honey

¼ cup cider vinegar

½ teaspoon salt

½ teaspoon dried sage

½ teaspoon dried rosemary

½ teaspoon freshly ground black pepper

Three 19-ounce cans red kidney beans or pinto beans, rinsed and drained

1. In a large nonstick skillet, heat the oil until hot but not smoking over medium heat. Add the bacon and cook until lightly crisped, about 2 minutes. With a slotted spoon, transfer the bacon to a plate. Add the pork chops to the pan in batches and cook until browned, about 2 minutes per side. With a slotted spoon, transfer the chops to the plate with the bacon.

2. Preheat the oven to 400°. Add the onions, garlic, and ginger to the pan and cook, stirring frequently, until the onions are softened, about 7 minutes. Add the carrots and Italian peppers, stirring to coat. Cook until the carrots are tender, about 5 minutes.

3. Stir in the tomatoes with their juices, the tomato sauce, honey, and vinegar. Increase the heat to medium-high and bring to a boil. Reduce to a simmer, cover, and cook until the flavors have blended, about 4 minutes longer. Stir in the salt, sage, rosemary, and black pepper and return the mixture to a boil.

4. Spoon the tomato mixture into a 4-quart baking dish and stir in the beans and bacon until well combined. Add the chops, spooning the beans over, cover with foil, and bake for 25 minutes, or until the beans are bubbly and the chops are cooked through. Divide the baked beans and chops among 8 plates and serve.

Suggested accompaniment: Spinach salad with a soy-ginger vinaigrette.

FAT: 14G/26%
CALORIES: 481
SATURATED FAT: 4G
CARBOHYDRATE: 60G
PROTEIN: 32G
CHOLESTEROL: 58MG
SODIUM: 538MG

For this hearty dish we use the long, tapered, Italian frying peppers, milder than our usual bell peppers.

Cider vinegar adds a nice bite to the lean lamb filling, while low-fat cottage cheese and skim milk thickened with a little flour create the rich-tasting, cheesy topping in this Greek favorite. A final dusting of Parmesan followed by a quick run under the broiler imparts an appetizing, golden glow. Small macaroni, bow ties, or ziti may be substituted for the shells.

PASTITSIO

SERVES: 8
WORKING TIME: 30 MINUTES
TOTAL TIME: 1 HOUR 10 MINUTES

16 ounces small pasta shells

2 teaspoons olive oil

1 medium onion, chopped

2 cloves garlic, minced

*1 pound lean ground lamb
(see tip)*

*¾ pound eggplant, peeled and
cut into ½-inch cubes*

¼ cup dark raisins or currants

1½ teaspoons dried oregano

¾ teaspoon salt

½ teaspoon cinnamon

*Two 8-ounce cans no-salt-added
tomato sauce*

2 teaspoons cider vinegar

1 cup skim milk

3 tablespoons flour

*1½ cups low-fat (1%) cottage
cheese*

¼ teaspoon white pepper

¼ cup grated Parmesan cheese

*1 tablespoon chopped fresh
parsley*

1. In a large pot of boiling water, cook the pasta until just tender. Drain well and set aside. Meanwhile, in a large nonstick skillet, heat the oil until hot but not smoking over medium heat. Add the onion and garlic and cook, stirring frequently, until the onion is softened, about 7 minutes. Add the lamb, eggplant, raisins, 1¼ teaspoons of the oregano, the salt, and cinnamon and cook, stirring frequently, until the lamb is browned, about 12 minutes. Remove from the heat and stir in the tomato sauce and vinegar. Set aside.

2. Meanwhile, preheat the oven to 400°. In a blender or food processor, purée the milk and flour until smooth. Transfer to a small saucepan, bring to a boil over medium heat, and cook, whisking constantly, until the mixture is slightly thickened, about 4 minutes. Remove from the heat. In a blender or food processor, purée the cottage cheese, pepper, and remaining ¼ teaspoon oregano until smooth. Stir the cheese purée into the milk mixture until combined.

3. Spray a 3-quart baking dish with nonstick cooking spray. Spoon half of the pasta into the prepared dish and top with half of the lamb mixture. Repeat with the remaining pasta and lamb. Spoon the white sauce over, cover with foil, and bake for 30 minutes. Preheat the broiler. Remove the foil, sprinkle the Parmesan over, and broil for 3 minutes, or until golden. Sprinkle with the parsley and serve.

Suggested accompaniment: Strawberries rolled in confectioners' sugar.

FAT: 8G/16%
CALORIES: 421
SATURATED FAT: 2.4G
CARBOHYDRATE: 60G
PROTEIN: 28G
CHOLESTEROL: 42MG
SODIUM: 500MG

TIP

To grind your own lamb at home, purchase a pound of lean, boneless lamb. Cut into ¼-inch cubes and place in a food processor. Process the lamb with on-off pulses until finely ground, scraping down the sides of the bowl with a rubber spatula as needed.

This country-kitchen classic highlights chicken bathed in a rich purée of root vegetables, made robust with sweet cooked garlic squeezed from the cloves. The dark meat of the chicken leg adds to the flavor (but we've removed the skin to economize on the fat). Any extra broth can be refrigerated or frozen for extra use.

CHICKEN IN A POT

SERVES: 8
WORKING TIME: 25 MINUTES
TOTAL TIME: 1 HOUR 5 MINUTES

*6 carrots, cut into 2-inch
pieces*

*4 leeks, halved lengthwise and
cut into 2-inch pieces*

4 turnips, quartered

*1 whole bulb garlic, loose papery
outer skin removed (do not
separate cloves)*

2 bay leaves

1 tablespoon fresh lemon juice

1¼ teaspoons salt

1 teaspoon dried tarragon

¾ teaspoon dried thyme

*½ teaspoon freshly ground black
pepper*

*8 whole chicken legs (about
4 pounds total), skinned*

*2 pounds all-purpose potatoes,
peeled and cut into 1½-inch
chunks*

*2 zucchini, cut into thin
diagonal slices*

1. In a large Dutch oven, combine the carrots, leeks, turnips, garlic, bay leaves, lemon juice, ¾ teaspoon of the salt, the tarragon, thyme, and pepper. Add water to cover by 3 inches and bring to a boil over high heat. Add the chicken, potatoes, and if necessary, enough water to just cover. Return to a boil, skimming off any foam. Reduce to a simmer, cover, and cook for 20 minutes.

2. Stir in the zucchini. Cover again and cook until the vegetables are tender and the chicken is cooked through, about 10 minutes longer. Strain the broth through a fine sieve into a large bowl and skim off any fat from the surface. Remove the garlic bulb and refrigerate until cool enough to handle. Discard the bay leaves.

3. In a food processor, combine 3 cups of the broth and 2 cups of the cooked vegetables. Slice off the top quarter inch of the garlic bulb to expose the pulp (see tip; top photo). Squeeze out the softened pulp (bottom photo) and add to the food processor along with the remaining ½ teaspoon salt. Purée until the mixture is smooth.

4. Divide the chicken and remaining vegetables among 8 shallow bowls, spoon the garlic-vegetable purée on top, and serve with the remaining broth.

*Suggested accompaniments: Sourdough baguette. Follow with peach halves
drizzled with honey and broiled, then sprinkled with dried cranberries.*

FAT: 5G/15%
CALORIES: 318
SATURATED FAT: 1.3G
CARBOHYDRATE: 37G
PROTEIN: 31G
CHOLESTEROL: 104MG
SODIUM: 530MG

TIP

*To extract the cooked,
sweet garlic pulp from the
whole bulb of garlic, snip
off the top ¼ inch of the
bulb with kitchen scissors.
Gently squeeze the sides of
the cloves to force out the
cooked pulp, and then add
to the vegetable mixture in
the food processor.*

BROCCOLI-MUSHROOM LASAGNA

SERVES: 8
WORKING TIME: 35 MINUTES
TOTAL TIME: 1 HOUR 30 MINUTES

Although this lasagna tastes rich, it's remarkably low in fat since we've used one-percent cottage cheese and reduced-fat cream cheese (Neufchâtel), mixed with grated Parmesan for a flavor boost. If desired, assemble the lasagna a day ahead, cover, and refrigerate until you're ready to bake. Be sure to let the lasagna stand for fifteen minutes before cutting so the slices will be firmer.

20 lasagna noodles

3 cups sliced mushrooms

1 cup shredded carrots

3 cloves garlic, minced

½ teaspoon dried rosemary

Two 10-ounce packages frozen chopped broccoli, thawed and drained

16-ounce can no-salt-added whole tomatoes, drained and coarsely chopped

Two 16-ounce containers low-fat (1%) cottage cheese

3 ounces reduced-fat cream cheese (Neufchâtel)

2 egg whites

¼ cup grated Parmesan cheese

¼ teaspoon white pepper

Two 8-ounce cans no-salt-added tomato sauce

14½-ounce can no-salt-added stewed tomatoes, chopped with their juices

¼ cup no-salt-added tomato paste

1 teaspoon dried basil

8 ounces part-skim mozzarella cheese, shredded (about 2 cups)

1. In a large pot of boiling water, cook the noodles until almost tender. Drain. Transfer to a bowl of cold water to prevent sticking. Meanwhile, spray a large nonstick skillet with nonstick cooking spray, then place over medium-high heat. Add the mushrooms, carrots, garlic, and rosemary and cook, stirring, until the mushrooms are tender, about 5 minutes. Add the broccoli and tomatoes and cook until the liquid evaporates, about 6 minutes. Set aside.

2. Preheat the oven to 400°. In a blender or food processor, purée the cottage cheese, cream cheese, egg whites, 2 tablespoons of the Parmesan, and the pepper until smooth. In a medium bowl, stir together the tomato sauce, stewed tomatoes, tomato paste, and basil.

3. In a 13 x 9-inch baking dish, spread ½ cup of the tomato sauce. Lay 4 lasagna noodles on top, overlapping slightly. Spoon one-third of the cheese purée, then one-third of the vegetables over. Top with 4 noodles and 1½ cups sauce. Sprinkle 1 cup of the mozzarella over. Top with 4 more noodles, another one-third of the purée, and one-third of the vegetables. Top with 4 noodles. Add the remaining purée, vegetables, and noodles. Spoon the remaining sauce over. Cover with foil and bake for 40 minutes. Remove the foil, sprinkle the remaining 1 cup mozzarella and 2 tablespoons Parmesan over, and bake for 15 minutes longer, or until the cheese is melted.

Suggested accompaniment: Fresh fruit cup with vanilla nonfat yogurt.

FAT: 11G/19%
CALORIES: 518
SATURATED FAT: 5.8G
CARBOHYDRATE: 70G
PROTEIN: 37G
CHOLESTEROL: 31MG
SODIUM: 756MG

CHOUCROUTE GARNI

SERVES: 8
WORKING TIME: 55 MINUTES
TOTAL TIME: 1 HOUR 30 MINUTES

This trim version of the traditional Alsatian cold-weather casserole requires a bit of time, but the impressive results are worth it.

4 teaspoons paprika

4 cloves garlic, minced, plus 4 cloves garlic, slivered

2 bay leaves, crushed

½ teaspoon ground allspice

8 thin bone-in center-cut loin pork chops (4 ounces each)

2 teaspoons olive oil

2 large onions, thinly sliced

5 carrots, thinly sliced

4 McIntosh apples, cored and cut into large dice

1 cup dry white wine or apple cider

1 small head cabbage, thinly sliced

2½ pounds red potatoes, halved if small, quartered if large

1 pound sauerkraut, rinsed and drained

3 tablespoons cider vinegar

½ teaspoon freshly ground black pepper

4 ounces turkey sausage or chicken hot dogs, thickly sliced

1 tablespoon chopped fresh parsley

1. In a small bowl, combine the paprika, minced garlic, bay leaves, and allspice. Rub the mixture into the pork chops on both sides. In a large Dutch oven, heat the oil until hot but not smoking over medium heat. Add the chops in batches and cook until browned, about 2 minutes per side. With a slotted spatula, transfer the chops to a large roasting pan and set aside.

2. Add the onions, slivered garlic, and ½ cup of water to the Dutch oven and cook, stirring frequently, until the onions are golden brown, about 10 minutes. Add the carrots and cook until tender, about 5 minutes. Stir in the apples. Add ½ cup of the wine, cover, and cook until the apples are tender, about 5 minutes.

3. Stir in the cabbage, potatoes, sauerkraut, remaining ½ cup wine, the vinegar, and pepper. Cover again and cook, stirring occasionally, until the potatoes are tender, about 20 minutes longer.

4. Meanwhile, preheat the oven to 425°. Stir the sausage into the cabbage mixture, then spoon the mixture over the chops. Cover with foil, place in the oven, and bake for 15 minutes, or until the chops and sausage are cooked through and the cabbage mixture is piping hot. Divide the chops and cabbage mixture among 8 plates, sprinkle with the parsley, and serve.

Suggested accompaniments: Chilled white wine, and seeded rye bread.

FAT: 14/29%
CALORIES: 446
SATURATED FAT: 4G
CARBOHYDRATE: 52G
PROTEIN: 24G
CHOLESTEROL: 64MG
SODIUM: 311MG

Spaghetti with Chunky Turkey Sausage Sauce

SERVES: 12
WORKING TIME: 35 MINUTES
TOTAL TIME: 1 HOUR

1 tablespoon olive oil

1½ pounds turkey sausage, casings removed, cut into ½-inch-thick slices

2 large onions, cut into 1-inch chunks

6 cloves garlic, minced

4 carrots, cut into ½-inch-thick slices

1 pound mushrooms, quartered

3½ pounds plum tomatoes, coarsely chopped

Three 8-ounce cans tomato sauce

2 teaspoons dried oregano

1 teaspoon salt

2 pounds spaghetti

2 zucchini, cut into ½-inch chunks

1. In a large Dutch oven, heat the oil until hot but not smoking over medium heat. Add the sausage and cook, stirring frequently, until browned and cooked through, about 7 minutes. With a slotted spoon, transfer the sausage to a plate and set aside.

2. Add the onions and garlic to the pan and cook, stirring frequently, until the onions are golden brown, about 10 minutes. Add the carrots and cook until the carrots are tender, about 7 minutes. Add the mushrooms and cook until the mushrooms are tender, about 5 minutes. Stir in the tomatoes, tomato sauce, oregano, and salt and bring to a boil. Return the sausage to the pan. Reduce to a simmer, cover, and cook until the sauce is slightly thickened, about 15 minutes.

3. Meanwhile, in a large pot of boiling water, cook the spaghetti until just tender. Drain, return to the cooking pot, and cover to keep warm.

4. Stir the zucchini into the sauce. Cover again and cook until the zucchini is just tender, 5 to 7 minutes longer. Pour the sauce over the spaghetti and toss well to combine. Divide the spaghetti mixture among 12 shallow bowls and serve.

Suggested accompaniments: Garlic bread. For dessert, sliced navel oranges topped with a strawberry purée.

FAT: 9G/18%
CALORIES: 471
SATURATED FAT: 2.1G
CARBOHYDRATE: 77G
PROTEIN: 23G
CHOLESTEROL: 30MG
SODIUM: 927MG

You can easily freeze half of the savory sauce for another party and then reheat it, tossing it with a pound of pasta.

PEASANT-STYLE BEEF STEW

SERVES: 8
WORKING TIME: 40 MINUTES
TOTAL TIME: 1 HOUR 30 MINUTES

Strongly flavored with sage, thyme, and a generous splash of red wine, this homey stew satisfies even the most ravenous appetites with just three ounces of meat per serving, thanks to lots of vegetables and beans. Enjoy your own party by preparing this a day or two ahead— then place the stew, reheated in an attractive kettle, on a buffet table with a stack of serving bowls.

¼ cup plus 3 tablespoons flour

½ teaspoon salt

¼ teaspoon freshly ground black pepper

1½ pounds top round of beef, cut into ½-inch cubes

1 tablespoon olive oil

3 cloves garlic, minced

1 pound carrots, thickly sliced

Two 14½-ounce cans reduced-sodium beef broth, defatted

1 cup dry red wine

2 tablespoons tomato paste

2 teaspoons dried sage

1 teaspoon dried thyme

1 teaspoon dry mustard

1½ pounds small red potatoes, quartered

10 ounces mushrooms, quartered

10-ounce package frozen pearl onions, thawed

16-ounce can red kidney beans or chick-peas, rinsed and drained

¼ cup chopped fresh parsley

1. In a shallow bowl, combine ¼ cup of the flour, the salt, and pepper. Add half of the beef and dredge in the flour mixture, shaking off the excess. In a large Dutch oven, heat half of the oil until hot but not smoking over medium heat. Add the floured beef and cook, stirring frequently, until browned, about 8 minutes. Transfer to a plate. Repeat with the remaining beef, flour mixture, and oil.

2. Return all the beef to the pan. Stir in the garlic, carrots, broth, wine, tomato paste, sage, thyme, and mustard and bring to a boil. Reduce to a simmer, cover, and cook, stirring occasionally, until the flavors have blended, about 15 minutes.

3. Stir in the potatoes, mushrooms, and onions. Cover again and cook until the potatoes and beef are tender, about 20 minutes. Stir in the beans and parsley and cook, uncovered, until the beans are heated through, about 3 minutes.

4. In a jar with a tight-fitting lid, combine the remaining 3 tablespoons flour and ¼ cup of water, shake until smooth, and stir into the simmering stew. Cook, stirring constantly, until the stew is slightly thickened, about 2 minutes longer.

Suggested accompaniments: Crusty rolls, followed by chunky applesauce with dried currants and a dusting of cinnamon.

FAT: 11G/28%
CALORIES: 360
SATURATED FAT: 3.4G
CARBOHYDRATE: 39G
PROTEIN: 26G
CHOLESTEROL: 52MG
SODIUM: 585MG

CREOLE TURKEY AND RICE STEW

SERVES: 8
WORKING TIME: 25 MINUTES
TOTAL TIME: 55 MINUTES

In our simple version of this Southern favorite, we use okra to thicken the stew. Green peppers add a smokier flavor than the sweeter red (or yellow) peppers, so be sure not to replace them with the other colors. Surprisingly, just a tiny amount of baked ham lends a deeply rich taste. Leftovers are easily reheated on the stovetop or in the microwave.

1 tablespoon olive oil
4 ribs celery, chopped
2 green bell peppers, chopped
1 red bell pepper, chopped
1 large red onion, chopped
1½ teaspoons dried thyme
1 teaspoon dried oregano
Two 14½-ounce cans reduced-sodium chicken broth, defatted
16-ounce can no-salt-added whole tomatoes, coarsely chopped with their juices
3 ounces baked ham, cut into ¼-inch cubes
1¼ cups long-grain rice
10-ounce package frozen cut okra
Two 10-ounce packages frozen corn kernels
10-ounce package frozen lima beans
1½ pounds turkey breast, cut into ¾-inch cubes
2 teaspoons Worcestershire sauce
½ to 1 teaspoon hot pepper sauce

1. In a large Dutch oven, heat the oil until hot but not smoking over medium-high heat. Add the celery, bell peppers, and onion and cook, stirring frequently, until the vegetables are softened, about 8 minutes. Add the thyme and oregano and cook, stirring constantly, until well coated, about 2 minutes.

2. Stir in the broth, 2 cups of water, the tomatoes with their juices, ham, and rice. Bring to a boil, reduce to a simmer, and cook, stirring occasionally, until the flavors have blended, about 10 minutes.

3. Stir in the okra, increase the heat to medium, and cook for 5 minutes. Stir in the corn, lima beans, and turkey and cook until the rice is tender and the turkey is cooked through, 5 to 10 minutes longer. Stir in the Worcestershire sauce and hot pepper sauce. Ladle the stew into 8 shallow bowls and serve.

Suggested accompaniments: Chicory and watercress salad drizzled with a buttermilk dressing. For dessert, bananas sautéed with brown sugar and almond liqueur.

FAT: 4G/10%
CALORIES: 388
SATURATED FAT: .9G
CARBOHYDRATE: 56G
PROTEIN: 33G
CHOLESTEROL: 59MG
SODIUM: 563MG

Southern-Style Shrimp Boil

SERVES: 8
WORKING TIME: 10 MINUTES
TOTAL TIME: 45 MINUTES

4 bay leaves

½ teaspoon whole allspice

½ teaspoon coriander seeds

½ teaspoon yellow mustard seeds

2 cups bottled clam juice or reduced-sodium chicken broth, defatted

1 cup sliced scallions

½ cup sliced celery

¾ teaspoon salt

½ teaspoon red pepper flakes

2 pounds small red potatoes, halved if large

4 ears corn, husks removed, cut in half

3 pounds large unpeeled shrimp

8 cups coarsely torn spinach leaves

1. Make a bouquet garni by combining the bay leaves, allspice, coriander, and mustard seeds on a square of cheesecloth, gathering the cheesecloth ends, and tying with string. In a large pot, combine the bouquet garni, clam juice, 6 cups of water, the scallions, celery, salt, and red pepper flakes. Bring to a boil over high heat.

2. Add the potatoes and return to a boil. Reduce to a simmer, cover, and cook until the potatoes are tender, about 25 minutes.

3. Stir in the corn, shrimp, and spinach. Cover again and cook until the shrimp are just opaque and the corn is tender, about 7 minutes longer. Discard the bouquet garni and serve.

Suggested accompaniments: Limeade, herbed biscuits, and chocolate or vanilla ice milk for dessert.

FAT: 3G/10%
CALORIES: 299
SATURATED FAT: .6G
CARBOHYDRATE: 34G
PROTEIN: 34G
CHOLESTEROL: 210MG
SODIUM: 608MG

Try to use the more mildly flavored Turkish bay leaves for the best taste in this wonderfully informal dish. If you have ground spices rather than seeds in the cupboard, skip the bouquet garni and add the ground allspice and coriander directly to the pot, omitting the mustard seeds. Cooking the shrimp in their shells enriches the broth—be sure to furnish plenty of napkins.

Keeping the meatballs small stretches less than a pound of meat to feed a crowd. And we avoid adding extra fat by baking the meatballs, rather than sautéing them in oil. Fresh dill is essential, both in the meatballs and as the final garnish. Store dill in the refrigerator with the stems in a glass of water and the tops covered with a plastic bag.

Swedish Meatballs

SERVES: 8
WORKING TIME: 30 MINUTES
TOTAL TIME: 50 MINUTES

2 cups fresh bread crumbs (see tip)

⅓ cup skim milk

¾ pound lean ground beef

3 scallions, finely chopped

2 egg whites

3 teaspoons snipped fresh dill

¾ teaspoon dry mustard

12 ounces yolk-free egg noodles

14½-ounce can reduced-sodium beef broth, defatted

1 tablespoon tomato paste

1 teaspoon paprika

½ teaspoon salt

1 red or yellow bell pepper, cut into thin slivers

Half medium red onion, cut into thin slivers

1 zucchini, cut into 2-inch julienne

3 tablespoons flour

½ cup reduced-fat sour cream

1½ tablespoons fresh lemon juice

1. Preheat the oven to 400°. Line a baking sheet with foil. In a large bowl, combine the bread crumbs and milk. Add the beef, scallions, egg whites, 1 teaspoon of the dill, and the mustard and mix until well combined. Using a rounded teaspoon for each, form the mixture into 32 small meatballs. Place on the prepared baking sheet and bake for 10 minutes, or until the meatballs are cooked through.

2. Meanwhile, in a large pot of boiling water, cook the noodles until just tender. Drain well.

3. In a medium saucepan, stir together the broth, tomato paste, paprika, and salt. Bring to a simmer over medium heat, add the bell pepper and onion, and cook for 4 minutes. Add the zucchini and cook until the pepper and onion are crisp-tender, about 4 minutes.

4. In a jar with a tight-fitting lid, shake together the flour and ¼ cup of water until smooth. Whisk the flour mixture into the broth mixture and cook, whisking constantly, until the sauce comes to a simmer. Add the meatballs and cook until heated through, about 3 minutes longer. Remove from the heat and stir in the sour cream and lemon juice. Divide the noodles and meatballs among 8 shallow bowls, sprinkle the remaining 2 teaspoons dill on top, and serve.

Suggested accompaniments: Sliced cucumber salad with a horseradish and parsley vinaigrette. For dessert, assorted reduced-fat cookies.

FAT: 8G/22%
CALORIES: 315
SATURATED FAT: 3G
CARBOHYDRATE: 43G
PROTEIN: 20G
CHOLESTEROL: 32MG
SODIUM: 409MG

TIP

To make fresh bread crumbs, tear the bread into pieces and place in a food processor. Process the bread with on-off pulses until finely ground and fluffy. If not using right away, place the bread crumbs in a freezer bag, press out the air, seal, and freeze for several months.

GLOSSARY

Almond—The seed of the sweet almond tree. Almonds are sold whole, slivered, and sliced. Whole almonds sold with their papery brown skins are generally labeled "natural." Almonds that have been skinned are called "blanched." Slivered almonds are always blanched, and sliced almonds generally still have the skins on (for a more attractive appearance). Use almonds sparingly since nuts add fat. Store in the freezer for up to 1 year.

Basil—An herb with a flavor between clove and licorice. Fresh basil will retain more fragrance if added at the end of cooking; dried basil is much milder, but can still be used to advantage in soups and stews. To store fresh basil, refrigerate, unwashed, with the stem ends in a jar of water and the tops covered with a plastic bag, for up to 3 days.

Basmati rice—An aromatic, long-grain rice with a nutty flavor and fragrance, available both white and brown. Grown primarily in northern India and Pakistan, basmati rice is aged, which causes the cooked grains to remain dry and separate. Buy the rice at Middle Eastern food shops and in the rice section of your supermarket.

Barley, pearl—Barley grain stripped of the husk and embryo, then steamed and polished, making it relatively quick cooking. It comes in three sizes: coarse, medium, and fine, and is especially delicious in soups.

Bay leaf—The dried, whole leaf of the evergreen European laurel tree. The herb adds a distinctive, pungent flavor to soups, stews, and casseroles; the Turkish variety is milder in flavor than other types.

Buttermilk—A milk product made by adding a special bacterial culture to nonfat or lowfat milk. Buttermilk lends a tangy taste and aroma, a slightly thickened texture, and a flavorful richness to soups, stews, casseroles, and sauces without significant extra fat. Use within 1 week of purchase, or substitute dry buttermilk powder (which has a much longer shelf life), following the directions on the package. In a pinch, make your own "buttermilk" by combining 1 tablespoon lemon juice or vinegar with enough milk to make 1 cup.

Cauliflower—A member of the cabbage family, typically creamy white, although there are purple and green varieties. Select blemish-free heads with fresh green leaves, and sniff—there should be no cabbagy smell. Refrigerate, unwashed, in a perforated plastic bag for a day or two. This vegetable works well in highly seasoned dishes, such as curries, since it absorbs flavors and provides crunchy texture.

Cayenne pepper—A spice ground from dried red chili peppers. Cayenne adds heat to chilis, stir-fries, casseroles, or any other dish where you desire a lively flavor.

Cheddar cheese—A semi-hard cow's milk cheese that can range in flavor from mild to very sharp, and in color from creamy white to pumpkin orange. It adds richness and smoothness to casseroles, but should be used sparingly since it is high in fat. With the strongly flavored sharp Cheddars, a little will go a long way. (Reduced-fat Cheddar will not melt as well.) Refrigerate, well wrapped, for up to 3 weeks.

Chutney—A sweet, spicy condiment ranging from smooth to chunky, generally made of fruit and spices. Chutney is most often used in Indian cooking, especially as an accompaniment to curries.

Clam, littleneck—A small, hard-shell clam, less than 2 inches in diameter, found along the Atlantic Coast. Its delicate flavor and texture is ideal for fish stews and soups or sautés. Purchase only live clams: those with tightly closed shells or whose slightly opened shells immediately close when tapped. Use as soon after buying as possible; refrigerate no more than a day or two.

Coriander—A spice made from the seeds of the coriander plant. They have a more citrusy flavor than the plant's leaves, which are also known as cilantro. Coriander is most often sold ground, but is also available as whole seeds.

Crabmeat—The meat from various varieties of hard-shell crabs, the tastiest part being from lump or backfin meat. Crab is most conveniently purchased in "lump" form, which is meat picked from the crab, cleaned, cooked, and packed fresh or frozen. Crabmeat can also be purchased canned, but the canned is often flaked meat and is not as flavorful. Add crabmeat toward the end of the cooking time, since overcooking makes it tough.

Cream cheese, reduced-fat—A light cream cheese, commonly called Neufchâtel, with about one-third less fat than regular cream cheese. It can always be used as a substitute for regular cream cheese. A small amount used in casseroles duplicates the richness of full-fat cheese or heavy cream.

Cumin—A peppery-tasting spice essential to many Middle Eastern, Asian, Mexican, and Mediterranean dishes. It is available ground or as whole seeds.

Dutch oven—A large saucepot or flameproof casserole with ear handles and a tight-fitting cover; useful for both stovetop and oven cooking. For the recipes in this book, use a Dutch oven with a 4- to 6-quart capacity that has been treated with a nonstick coating.

Evaporated milk, skimmed and low-fat—Canned, unsweetened, homogenized milk that has had more than half of its water and most of its fat removed: In the skimmed version, 100 percent of the fat has been removed; the low-fat version contains 1 percent fat. Added to casseroles, it adds a creamy richness with almost no fat. Store at room temperature for up to 6 months until opened, and then refrigerate for up to 1 week.

Fennel—A vegetable resembling celery that brings both crunch and a subtle licorice flavor to a variety of dishes. The feathery tops of the fennel plant (called fronds) are used as an herb; the bulb is used raw or cooked in salads or casseroles, and the seeds are frequently used to season sauces, especially pasta sauces. Choose fennel with bulbs that are crisp and stalks that have bright green fronds. Store in the refrigerator, in a plastic bag, for a day or two.

Feta cheese—A soft, crumbly, cured Greek cheese, traditionally made from sheep's or goat's milk. White and rindless, feta is usually available as a square packed in its own brine, and can be recognized in a dish by its somewhat salty, tangy flavor. Use sparingly in casseroles for bold flavor and rich texture, without excessive fat.

Green chilies, canned—The pungent, pod-shaped fruit of various chili pepper plants, ranging from exceptionally hot to quite mild. Many varieties are available fresh, but canned chilies tend to be either jalapeños (see below) or those simply labeled "mild." Use the mild green chilies—which come whole or chopped—to add a subtly piquant green chili flavor to soups, stews, and casseroles.

 Green split pea—A field pea that has been dried and split. Split peas require no presoaking and simmer to tenderness in about 30 minutes. Use them to add body and a creamy texture to hearty soups and stews. Also available in a yellow variety.

Jalapeño pepper, pickled—The pickled version of the familiar hot chili pepper. It can be stored in the refrigerator for up to 6 months. As with fresh chilies, remove the seeds and membranes for less heat. Use just a small amount in a casserole for big flavor.

Leek—A member of the onion family that resembles a giant scallion. To prepare, trim the root end and any blemished dark green ends. Split lengthwise from the root end to the top, leaving the root end intact, and then rinse thoroughly to remove any dirt trapped between the leaves. Use leeks in one-dish meals for their light, almost sweet, onion flavor.

Monterey jack cheese—A mild cheese made from whole or skim milk, originally produced in Monterey, California. It has a delicate flavor, similar to American Muenster. The cheese melts readily and, shredded into a casserole, gives a milky richness. Often used in Southwestern cooking to "cool" the heat of chili peppers.

Mozzarella cheese—A soft, fresh cheese with great melting properties, originally made from water buffalo's milk, but now more commonly made from cow's milk, available both in whole milk and part-skim milk varieties. Its mild flavor can be used to good advantage in strongly flavored casseroles.

Mustard, dry—A spice ground from mustard seeds. Dry mustard powder ranges from mild to hot in flavor, and is often used in curries and dishes rich with cheese. The English-style variety, the most common, is made from yellow seeds and is mildly hot. Store in a cool, dark place for up to 6 months.

Napa cabbage—A member of the cabbage family, identified particularly with Chinese cooking. Napa cabbage has broad white ribs and frilly, light green tops, with a slightly sweet, much milder flavor than regular cabbage. Look for heads with firm leaves and no blemished edges. To store, refrigerate, unwashed, in a plastic bag for up to 1 week. Napa cabbage adds crunch and subtle green color to skillet or stir-fried dishes.

Noodles, egg—Egg noodles are distinct from pasta because eggs have been added to the basic concoction of flour and water. Yolk-free egg noodles are nutritionally smart, since, by removing the yolk, practically all the fat and cholesterol disappears. Use these noodles to add body to a dish and to soak up sauces.

Olive, green—Small, oval unripened fruit of the olive tree, available in dozens of varieties from most parts of the world. Green olives have a salty, tart taste. Before green olives can be eaten, they must first be brine-, oil-, or dry-cured to remove the bitterness. Chopped, sliced, or added whole, their presence is recognized by a distinctive earthy flavor. Use sparingly since olives, whether brine- or dry-cured, contain fat and salt, the latter from processing.

Orzo—A rice-shaped pasta, excellent for giving soups and stews a creamy body. Use as a delicious alternative to rice.

Paprika—A spice ground from red peppers and used in many traditional Hungarian and Spanish preparations. Paprika colors foods a characteristic brick red and flavors dishes from sweet to spicy hot, depending on the pepper potency.

Parmesan cheese—A full-flavored, hard grating cheese, ideal for low-fat cooking because a little goes a long way. Genuine Italian Parmesan, stamped "Parmigiano-Reggiano" on the rind, is produced in the Emilia-Romagna region, and tastes richly nutty with a slight sweetness. Buy Parmesan in blocks and grate it as needed for best flavor and freshness.

Pepper, Italian frying—A long, tapered pepper, also called cubanelle, that is sweeter than a regular bell pepper, and ranges in color from yellow to red. Frying or sautéing enhances the sweet flavor.

Phyllo dough—A flaky dough associated with the cuisines of Greece and the Middle East. It is frequently used as a crust for pies, both savory and sweet, and for meat- and vegetable-stuffed pastries. Phyllo itself has almost no fat, but the butter liberally applied between the layers to keep them separate and crisp turns it into a high-fat dough. To reduce much of the fat, spray the layers with nonstick cooking spray.

Poultry seasoning—A prepared blend of herbs—usually a mix of thyme, sage, marjoram, and black pepper—that accents the flavor of poultry. Store airtight in a cool, dark place for up to 6 months.

Provolone cheese—A cow's milk Italian cheese that has a slightly salty, smoky flavor, and can range from mellow to sharp, depending on how long the cheese is aged. Layered into a casserole sparingly, the cheese adds a wonderful richness, or it can be sprinkled on top and lightly browned.

Red pepper flakes—A spice made from a variety of dried red chili peppers. Pepper flakes will permeate a stew or a casserole with a burst of heat and flavor during the cooking and eating. Begin with a pinch—you can always add more.

Ricotta cheese—A fresh, creamy white cheese, smoother than cottage cheese, with a slightly sweet flavor. Available in whole-milk and part-skim versions, ricotta is often used in stuffed pastas, and a little can be stirred into a sauce for added richness as well as creamy body. Refrigerate and use within 1 week.

Salsa—A spicy sauce, used in the cooking of Mexico and the Southwest, made from a mixture of raw or cooked ingredients, especially tomatoes, chilies, and cilantro. Familiar as a dip with tortilla chips, salsa is also useful as a low-fat flavor enhancer in casseroles.

Sauerkraut—A fermented mixture of shredded cabbage, salt, and spices that adds texture and a distinctive "sour" flavor to a dish. It is available fresh in some ethnic delicatessens, in plastic bags in the refrigerated section of the supermarket, and in jars and cans. To lessen its salty flavor, rinse well and drain before using.

Snow pea—A flat pea pod that is fully edible, even uncooked. Slightly sweet and very tender, snow peas need only quick cooking and add both crunch and color. Select crisp, bright green pods, and refrigerate in a plastic bag for up to 3 days. Remove papery tips and strings before using.

Sour cream—A soured dairy product, resulting from treating sweet cream with a lactic acid culture. Regular sour cream contains at least 18 percent milk fat; reduced-fat sour cream contains 4 percent fat; nonfat sour cream contains no fat. In cooking, the reduced-fat version can be substituted for regular sour cream, but the nonfat should be used cautiously since it behaves differently, especially in baking. To avoid curdling, do not subject sour cream to high heat.

Sweet potato—A tuber with sweet yellow or orange flesh, sometimes mistakenly called a yam. When added to soups, stews, or casseroles, sweet potatoes impart rich body and a distinctive orange color and add vitamin C and a good deal of beta carotene. Choose smooth-skinned potatoes with tapered ends and no blemishes; remember, the darker the skin, the sweeter the taste. Store in a cool, dark place for up to 1 week.

Tarragon—A potent, sweet herb with a licorice- or anise-like flavor. Dried tarragon loses its potency quickly; check for flavor intensity by crushing a little between your fingers and sniffing for the strong aroma. As with most herbs, you may substitute 1 teaspoon dried for every tablespoon of fresh.

Turkey sausage, hot—A spicy sausage filled with ground turkey meat. It can be used to great advantage in low-fat cooking since ground turkey is much lower in fat than the ground pork used in Italian hot sausage. It is available in links and patties, and also comes in a milder, sweeter version, similar to Italian sweet sausage.

Turnip, white—A winter root vegetable used in soups and stews for its bitter-sweet flavor and slight crunch. Available all year round, turnips have a peak season from October to February. Buy small turnips, with unblemished skins, as they will have the mildest flavor.

Zest—The very thin, outermost colored part of the rind of a lemon, lime, or orange that contains strongly flavored oils. Citrus zest imparts a unique and intense flavor that helps to compensate for the lack of flavorful fat. Remove the zest with a grater, citrus zester, or vegetable peeler.

INDEX

Antipasto Dinner, Skillet, 41
Asparagus Strata, 93

Barbecue-Sauced Steak with Vegetable
    Kebabs, 130
Beef
    Barbecue-Sauced Steak with Vegetable
        Kebabs, 130
    Beef and Barley Soup, 23
    Beef Goulash, 14
    Beef Pilaf, 63
    Beef Pot Pie in Phyllo, 117
    Chicken-Fried Steak Dinner, 38
    Chili Pie, 105
    Cuban-Style Beef Stew, 22
    Ground Beef Pasties with Chutney Sauce,
        114
    Louisiana Beef Stew with Dumplings, 13
    Meat Loaf Blue Plate Special, 79
    Peasant-Style Beef Stew, 147
    Quick Beef Chili, 30
    Shepherd's Pie, 106
    Stir-Fried Beef and Vegetables with Orzo, 42
    Swedish Meatballs, 153
Blue Plate Special, Meat Loaf, 79
Bouillabaisse, 11

Casseroles
    Asparagus Strata, 93
    Baked Rigatoni with Vegetables, 72
    Broccoli-Mushroom Lasagna, 143
    Choucroute Garni, 144

Creamy Penne, Bacon, and Vegetable
    Bake, 80
Golden Chicken and Corn Casserole, 90
Ham and Scalloped Potatoes, 98
Hearty Cassoulet, 82
Pastitsio, 139
Tuna-Noodle Bake, 100
Turkey Orloff Casserole, 94
Vegetarian Moussaka, 89
Wagon Wheels with Spinach-Basil Sauce, 97
Cassoulet, Hearty, 82
Chicken
    Chicken and Mushroom Stew, 27
    Chicken Enchiladas, 85
    Chicken in a Pot, 141
    Chicken with Peanut Sauce, 64
    Chunky Chicken and Vegetable Hash, 54
    Coq au Vin, 34
    Country-Style Chicken Fricassee, 21
    Couscous with Chicken and Vegetables, 39
    Golden Chicken and Corn Casserole, 90
    Hearty Cassoulet, 82
    Moroccan Chicken Stew with Lemon, 29
    Paper-Wrapped Chicken and Vegetables, 86
    Roast Chicken Dinner, 71
    Spicy Rice with Chicken and Vegetables, 58
Chicken-Fried Steak Dinner, 38
Chili
    Green Chili with Pork, 136
    Quick Beef Chili, 30
    Three-Bean Vegetable Chili, 133
Chili Pie, 105
Choucroute Garni, 144

Chowder, Peppery Fish and Corn, 16
Clams
    Mixed Shellfish Stew, 19
Coq au Vin, 34
Country-Style Chicken Fricassee, 21
Couscous with Chicken and Vegetables, 39
Crab
    Bouillabaisse, 11
Creole Turkey and Rice Stew, 149
Cuban-Style Beef Stew, 22
Curried Pork Stew, 28

Deep-Dish Pan Pizza, 127

Eggplant and Pesto Sandwiches,
    Open-Face, 75
Eggs
    Broccoli and Potato Frittata, 50
Enchiladas, Chicken, 85

Fish/shellfish. See also specific types
    Baked Salmon on a Bed of Vegetables, 77
    Bouillabaisse, 11
    Cod Fillets in Parchment, 102
    Fish Roll-Up Supper, 53
    Hot and Tangy Shrimp, 45
    Mixed Shellfish Stew, 19
    Peppery Fish and Corn Chowder, 16
    Seafood-Sausage Paella, 36
    Southern-Style Shrimp Boil, 150
    Tuna-Noodle Bake, 100
Fricassee, Country-Style Chicken, 21
Frittata, Broccoli and Potato, 50

Goulash, Beef, 14
Greek Spinach and Feta Pie, 108

Ham
    Ham and Scalloped Potatoes, 98
    Ham and Sweet Potato Sauté, 49
Hash, Chunky Chicken and Vegetable, 54

Italian Pasta-Vegetable Soup, 33

Lamb
    Lamb Meatballs with Spinach Fusilli, 61
    Pastitsio, 139
Lasagna, Broccoli-Mushroom, 143
Louisiana Beef Stew with Dumplings, 13

Manicotti, Stuffed, with Ham and
    Cheese, 135
Meat Loaf Blue Plate Special, 79
Meatballs
    Lamb Meatballs with Spinach Fusilli, 61
    Skillet Spaghetti and Meatballs, 57
    Swedish Meatballs, 153
Mexican-Style Pizza, 122
Milanese-Style Rice, 68
Moroccan Chicken Stew with Lemon, 29
Moussaka, Vegetarian, 89

Open-Face Eggplant and Pesto
    Sandwiches, 75

Paella, Seafood-Sausage, 36

Pasta
   Baked Rigatoni with Vegetables, 72
   Broccoli-Mushroom Lasagna, 143
   Couscous with Chicken and Vegetables, 39
   Creamy Penne, Bacon, and Vegetable Bake, 80
   Lamb Meatballs with Spinach Fusilli, 61
   Pastitsio, 139
   Skillet Spaghetti and Meatballs, 57
   Spaghetti with Chunky Turkey Sausage Sauce, 145
   Stir-Fried Beef and Vegetables with Orzo, 42
   Stuffed Manicotti with Ham and Cheese, 135
   Tuna-Noodle Bake, 100
   Wagon Wheels with Spinach-Basil Sauce, 97
Pasties, Ground Beef, with Chutney Sauce, 114
Pastitsio, 139
Peasant-Style Beef Stew, 147
Pies, savory. *See also* Pizza; Turnovers
   Beef Pot Pie in Phyllo, 117
   Chili Pie, 105
   Greek Spinach and Feta Pie, 108
   Pork and Apple Pot Pie, 119
   Potato-Topped Turkey Pie, 107
   Rice-Crusted Quiche Lorraine, 125
   Shepherd's Pie, 106
   Stromboli, 121
   Tamale Pie, 128
   Vegetable Pot Pie, 111
Pilaf, Beef, 63

Pizza
   Deep-Dish Pan Pizza, 127
   Mexican-Style Pizza, 122
   Rustic Pizza, 113
Pork
   Baked Beans and Pork Chops, 137
   Choucroute Garni, 144
   Curried Pork Stew, 28
   Green Chili with Pork, 136
   Pork "Un-Fried" Rice, 47
   Pork and Apple Pot Pie, 119
   Pork and Butternut Squash Sauté, 66
   Pork and Three-Pepper Stew, 24
   Pork with Potatoes and Artichokes, 78
Pot pie. *See Pies, savory*

Quiche Lorraine, Rice-Crusted, 125
Quick Beef Chili, 30

Rice
   Beef Pilaf, 63
   Milanese-Style Rice, 68
   Pork "Un-Fried" Rice, 47
   Seafood-Sausage Paella, 36
   Spicy Rice with Chicken and Vegetables, 58
Rigatoni, Baked, with Vegetables, 72

Salmon, Baked, on a Bed of Vegetables, 77
Sandwiches, Open-Face Eggplant and Pesto, 75
Scalloped Potatoes, Ham and, 98

Scallops
   Bouillabaisse, 11
Shepherd's Pie, 106
Shrimp
   Hot and Tangy Shrimp, 45
   Mixed Shellfish Stew, 19
   Southern-Style Shrimp Boil, 150
Soups. *See also Stews*
   Beef and Barley Soup, 23
   Italian Pasta-Vegetable Soup, 33
   Peppery Fish and Corn Chowder, 16
   Split Pea Soup with Smoked Turkey, 17
Southern-Style Shrimp Boil, 150
Spaghetti
   Skillet Spaghetti and Meatballs, 57
   Spaghetti with Chunky Turkey Sausage Sauce, 145
Split Pea Soup with Smoked Turkey, 17
Steak
   Barbecue-Sauced Steak with Vegetable Kebabs, 130
   Chicken-Fried Steak Dinner, 38
Stews
   Beef Goulash, 14
   Bouillabaisse, 11
   Chicken and Mushroom Stew, 27
   Coq au Vin, 34
   Country-Style Chicken Fricassee, 21
   Creole Turkey and Rice Stew, 149
   Cuban-Style Beef Stew, 22
   Curried Pork Stew, 28
   Green Chili with Pork, 136

   Louisiana Beef Stew with Dumplings, 13
   Mixed Shellfish Stew, 19
   Moroccan Chicken Stew with Lemon, 29
   Peasant-Style Beef Stew, 147
   Pork and Three-Pepper Stew, 24
   Quick Beef Chili, 30
   Three-Bean Vegetable Chili, 133
Strata, Asparagus, 93
Stromboli, 121
Swedish Meatballs, 153

Tamale Pie, 128
Tuna-Noodle Bake, 100
Turkey
   Creole Turkey and Rice Stew, 149
   Potato-Topped Turkey Pie, 107
   Split Pea Soup with Smoked Turkey, 17
   Tamale Pie, 128
   Turkey Orloff Casserole, 94
Turnovers
   Ground Beef Pasties with Chutney Sauce, 114

"Un-Fried" Rice, Pork, 47

Vegetarian Moussaka, 89

TIME LIFE BOOKS

Time-Life Books is a division of Time Life Inc.

PRESIDENT and CEO: John M. Fahey, Jr.

TIME-LIFE BOOKS

MANAGING EDITOR: Roberta Conlan

Director of Design: Michael Hentges
Director of Editorial Operations: Ellen Robling
Director of Photography and Research: John Conrad Weiser
Senior Editors: Russell B. Adams, Jr., Dale M. Brown, Janet Cave,
   Lee Hassig, Robert Somerville, Henry Woodhead
Director of Technology: Eileen Bradley
Library: Louise D. Forstall

PRESIDENT: John D. Hall

Vice President, Director of New Product Development: Neil Kagan
Associate Director, New Product Development: Quentin S. McAndrew
Marketing Director, New Product Development: Robin B. Shuster
Director of Finance: Christopher Hearing
Vice President, Book Production: Marjann Caldwell
Production Manager: Marlene Zack
Consulting Editor: Catherine Boland Hackett

Design for Great Taste-Low Fat by David Fridberg of
Miles Fridberg Molinaroli, Inc.

REBUS, INC.

PUBLISHER: Rodney M. Friedman
EDITORIAL DIRECTOR: Charles L. Mee

Editorial Staff for *One-Pot Meals*
Director, Recipe Development and Photography: Grace Young
Editorial Director: Kate Slate
Senior Recipe Developer: Sandra Rose Gluck
Recipe Developer: Paul Piccuito
Managing Editor: Janet Charatan
Production Editor: Susan Paige
Writer: David J. Ricketts
Nutritionists: Hill Nutrition Associates

Art Directors: Sara Bowman, Timothy Jeffs
Photographers: Lisa Koenig, Vincent Lee
Photographers' Assistants: Eugene DeLucie, Rainer Fehringer,
   Robert Presciutti, Val Steiner
Food Stylists: A.J. Battifarano, Roberta Rall, Karen Pickus,
   Andrea B. Swenson
Assistant Food Stylists: Catherine Chatham, Amy Lord, Ellie Ritt
Prop Stylist: Debrah Donahue

Library of Congress Cataloging-in-Publication Data

One-pot meals.
p.   cm. -- (Great taste, low fat)
Includes index.
ISBN 0-7835-4552-5 (alk. paper)
1. Casserole cookery. 2. Low-fat diet--Recipes. 3. Quick and easy
cookery. I. Time-Life Books. II. Series.
TX693.053   1995
641.8'21--dc20   95-35152
                                                                          CIP

Other Publications

THE TIME-LIFE COMPLETE GARDENER
HOME REPAIR AND IMPROVEMENT
JOURNEY THROUGH THE MIND AND BODY
WEIGHT WATCHERS® SMART CHOICE RECIPE COLLECTION
TRUE CRIME
THE AMERICAN INDIANS
THE ART OF WOODWORKING
LOST CIVILIZATIONS
ECHOES OF GLORY
THE NEW FACE OF WAR
HOW THINGS WORK
WINGS OF WAR
CREATIVE EVERYDAY COOKING
COLLECTOR'S LIBRARY OF THE UNKNOWN
CLASSICS OF WORLD WAR II
TIME-LIFE LIBRARY OF CURIOUS AND UNUSUAL FACTS
AMERICAN COUNTRY
VOYAGE THROUGH THE UNIVERSE
THE THIRD REICH
MYSTERIES OF THE UNKNOWN
TIME FRAME
FIX IT YOURSELF
FITNESS, HEALTH & NUTRITION
SUCCESSFUL PARENTING
HEALTHY HOME COOKING
UNDERSTANDING COMPUTERS
LIBRARY OF NATIONS
THE ENCHANTED WORLD
THE KODAK LIBRARY OF CREATIVE PHOTOGRAPHY
GREAT MEALS IN MINUTES
THE CIVIL WAR
PLANET EARTH
COLLECTOR'S LIBRARY OF THE CIVIL WAR
THE EPIC OF FLIGHT
THE GOOD COOK
WORLD WAR II
THE OLD WEST

*For information on and a full description of any of the Time-Life Books series
listed above, please call 1-800-621-7026 or write:*
Reader Information
Time-Life Customer Service
P.O. Box C-32068
Richmond, Virginia 23261-2068

METRIC CONVERSION CHARTS

VOLUME EQUIVALENTS
(fluid ounces/milliliters and liters)

US	Metric
1 tsp	5 ml
1 tbsp (½ fl oz)	15 ml
¼ cup (2 fl oz)	60 ml
⅓ cup	80 ml
½ cup (4 fl oz)	120 ml
⅔ cup	160 ml
¾ cup (6 fl oz)	180 ml
1 cup (8 fl oz)	240 ml
1 qt (32 fl oz)	950 ml
1 qt + 3 tbsps	1 L
1 gal (128 fl oz)	4 L

Conversion formula
Fluid ounces X 30 = milliliters
1000 milliliters = 1 liter

WEIGHT EQUIVALENTS
(ounces and pounds/grams and kilograms)

US	Metric
¼ oz	7 g
½ oz	15 g
¾ oz	20 g
1 oz	30 g
8 oz (½ lb)	225 g
12 oz (¾ lb)	340 g
16 oz (1 lb)	455 g
35 oz (2.2 lbs)	1 kg

Conversion formula
Ounces X 28.35 = grams
1000 grams = 1 kilogram

LINEAR EQUIVALENTS
(inches and feet/centimeters and meters)

US	Metric
¼ in	.75 cm
½ in	1.5 cm
¾ in	1 cm
1 in	2.5 cm
6 in	15 cm
12 in (1 ft)	30 cm
39 in	1 m

Conversion formula
Inches X 2.54 = centimeters
100 centimeters = 1 meter

TEMPERATURE EQUIVALENTS
(Fahrenheit/Celsius)

US	Metric
0° (freezer temperature)	-18°
32° (water freezes)	0°
98.6°	37°
180° (water simmers*)	82°
212° (water boils*)	100°
250° (low oven)	120°
350° (moderate oven)	175°
425° (hot oven)	220°
500° (very hot oven)	260°

*at sea level

Conversion formula
Degrees Fahrenheit minus
32 ÷ 1.8 = degrees Celsius